BODY OF EVIDENCE

A Deadly Trail of Treachery and Deceit

Bruce Hutchison, Ph.D.

Special thanks to my wife Nancy for her unending love, encouragement and support.

Thanks to Jackie Doyle and George Stephenson for their friendship and excellent editing.

TABLE OF CONTENTS

In the Beginning

Sometimes you turn a corner on an ordinary day and something grabs you by your shoulders and yanks you off course in a way that changes everything. You suddenly follow a new and unexpected path, not knowing where it will lead. The initial whiff of excitement blew across my cheeks as more an accusation than an innocent question.

"You do know he didn't write them?" Eleanor asked as she tapped her napkin on the side of her lips.

I clinked my butter knife on my plate and looked across the table, her gray eyes like that of a cat who'd just snared a claw in her victim.

"What do you mean, he didn't write them? Of course he wrote them."

"Believe what you want to believe," she said, laying her napkin back in her lap and stretching a smirk as if to say, if I wanted to stay naïve then that was up to me.

"*All* of them?" I asked, entangling myself further.

"Yes, the plays, the sonnets… How *could* he? He couldn't write," she nodded.

"Wait a minute. Maybe not all of them," I said, finding myself surprisingly defensive, as though I had a stake in the matter.

"Bruce," she said, lowering her forehead and prolonging my name as she always did when she was about to get *very* serious. "Listen to me. I'm telling you, the man was illiterate; he could hardly scratch his own initials. His parents couldn't write. *They* signed with an 'X.' There are legal documents…. His wife? *She* 'X'd. So did all his children."

I didn't say anything. What *could* I say?

Eleanor leaned across the table, candlelight dancing on her cheeks. "William Shakespeare?" she said. "The man who supposedly wrote a million-plus words, the most beautiful, brilliant words ever penned, and he couldn't scribble his own name? He didn't bother teaching his children how to write. Don't you find that odd?"

I was stunned. I had vaguely heard the speculation that Shakespeare hadn't written Shakespeare, but had never heard any facts, any details. For some reason, Eleanor's certainty stiffened my guard. Perhaps I wasn't prepared to give up what I had painstakingly been taught, what I thought I knew. Or maybe it was more than that. Maybe I didn't like being fooled by all those high school teachers and college professors. Maybe I didn't like *them* being fooled.

Eleanor, a Smithsonian librarian I'd dated for several months back in my bachelor days, ate her Maryland rockfish in silence, as though she had had this conversation before and knew I needed time to let the idea filter through and settle in.

"Would you like me to get you something?" she asked, apparently realizing that further discussion risked a sour ending to an otherwise pleasant evening.

"Something like *what?*"

"Something from the Institute."

Big mistake. We had planned a romantic weekend at a South Mountain B&B in the Maryland Appalachians the following month. When Eleanor carted along a sheath of monographs and manila folders, I spent two days with my nose buried in papers. It was a long drive home and two lunches before she forgave me. It might have taken less time if I hadn't tried to blame her. After all, I insisted over the phone, she was the one who brought the subject up. "Methinks you protest too much," she said. "I'm busy. Call me later."

The more I thought about it, at least initially, the more my mind swirled in disbelief. How could Shakespeare *not* have written the plays? Why wouldn't Shakespeare *be* Shakespeare? Don't most authors and playwrights emblazon their name on the front page of their work?

How could such an incredible falsehood slide down the centuries undetected and unchallenged? That seemed unbelievable. And, if it *was* true, *why* was it true? What conspirators lurked in the shadows behind such a monumental deception? What motivated them? It had to be more than one. Who, alone, could successfully perpetrate what amounted to the greatest literary conspiracy in history?

True or false, the case against William Shakespeare as playwright had at least convinced one bright Smithsonian researcher that the true authorship pointed in another direction. Trying to resolve unanswered questions disturbed my sleep and startled me awake from naps I took to compensate for lack of rest. I sprung up in bed at 3 AM one morning, clicked on the lamp and reread what Eleanor had brought me that weekend that turned more sour than romantic.

I remembered feeling defensive for William Shakespeare. Leave the poor fellow alone, I thought. But now it occurred to me, if Shakespeare didn't write the plays, why feel sorry for him – an uneducated nobody who somehow parlayed his illiteracy into taking credit as the greatest playwright in the English language? In a convoluted way, working from nothing, he was astoundingly successful.

What Eleanor started, I knew I had to finish, but where to begin?

Shakespeare's Solemn Glare

Normally, I would have begun online. But I was lucky enough to live close to one of the world's largest depository of books and information, so why not start pre-digital, with books stamped and bound from the same Guttenberg invention that stamped and printed Shakespeare's First Folio?

Early on a late-fall morning, after grabbing a quick breakfast and carrying along a flip top coffee mug, I drove into Washington D.C. by the back way. I skipped around jammed New York Avenue by cutting through Anacostia, circled the old RFK stadium and aimed my Miata straight down a Capital Street tunnel of oaks whose fall leaves floated down in front of me and scattered in my wake.

The initial passion I needed to energize the research surged through my veins as I pressed the accelerator a little closer to the floor than any responsible D.C. police officer could comfortably ignore. But Lady Luck rode with me that morning. The local constabulary had conspicuously parked their black-and-whites in front of Capital Street's only donut shop to fuel themselves before embarking on their daily duties.

I parked on the only empty two-hour spot I could find on South "A" Street, then walked the four blocks past the backside of the Supreme Court building and along the front of the Folger Shakespeare Library, a façade that seemed to stare at me with distain. How could Shakespeare, whoever he was, fool the Folger Shakespeare Library? Had Folger, whomever Folger was, been fooled? How many foolish librarians, academics, researcher, and scholars could there be? Maybe I was the fool on a fool's journey. I increasingly had my doubts, but as I turned the corner on 1st and headed for the Library of Congress, I told myself I had come this far, I had taken the first step, why not take the next?

As I stepped inside the second floor reading room, an elaborately painted dome soared 160 feet above me, driving me back into the hall to regain my equilibrium. As I eased inside again, I was still mesmerized. Eight marble columns supported the egg shaped dome with the same number of panels embedded in the dome's interior, each depicting an epoch in civilization beginning with Egypt, passing through Europe's classical period, and culminating with the Americas.

Teetering high above on a narrow rim, giant-size statues glared down at readers below, each representing a separate branch of classic learning -- Michelangelo for art, Beethoven for music and William Shakespeare for drama.

The Bard appeared as if he could easily lean forward and come crashing down on my head for having the audacity to question his authenticity.

I gathered my courage and stepped up to the information station directly beneath the dome. "I'm looking for information related to Shakespeare," I said when I stepped up to the counter. "Alternative authors. That sort of thing."

An attractive, fiftyish brunette raised an eyebrow as if she'd been over this territory before. "Five at a time," she said. "That could take a while."

Rediscovering the Known

The first five books of an eventual two-dozen plunked down on my desk less than fifteen minutes later. There would have been more if my research hadn't edged up to closing time.

It didn't take long to discover that Eleanor was far from alone in her Shakespeare authorship doubts. Speculation about alterative playwrights had surfaced as early as the mid-1700's, more than a century after William Shakespeare death in 1616. Well before that time, the plays had outlived their popularity. No new plays were performed. There were none. Their familiar characters – Macbeth, Hamlet, and Katherine in *Taming of the Shrew,* and all the rest -- had strode upon the stage, strutted their stuff and acknowledged their applause for over a quarter century. Younger 17th century audiences craved new plots

and characters. The works of emerging playwrights --
Thomas Dekker, Thomas Heywood, Philip Massinger, and
Richard Brome -- more often filled the post-Elizabethan
stage. The Shakespeare plays – at least those *attributed* to
Shakespeare – weren't entirely upstaged by the new
generation, but they did slide further down the playlist as
tastes changed and competition grew.

Then, suddenly and decisively, a final curtain
dropped and all the theaters remained dark for next
eighteen years. Long seen as unclean, unsavory and
unhealthy by the Puritans, who had finally succeeded in
controlling the English Parliament, the doors of the British
theater, in the spring of 1642, were posted with the
following decree:

BY ORDER OF THE CROWN
CLOSED UNTIL FURTHER NOTICE

According to one book on the Elizabethan theater,
the theaters' reflecting stage-candles weren't relit and their
doors reopened until Charles II's decree in1660, nearly
three generations after Shakespeare's death and long after
his plays had long become passé.

Resurrection

The Folger's Shakespeare Library dwelled in a
much smaller building across the street from the Library of
Congress, its bas-relief scenes of Shakespeare plays

greeting me as I passed along the front, entered by the theater-side entrance and nodded toward an impish statue of Puck, rubbing Puck's polished knee for luck on the journey ahead.

I had already done a little homework on the Folger's library and learned that Henry Clay Folger – a one-time president and chairman of the board of Standard Oil of New York – had dedicated much of his time, wealth, and energy to the design and construction of a building to house his accumulating collection of Shakespeare related material, including eighty-two copies of original First Folios and several earlier quartos of individual plays.

Anyone can buy a ticket to see a Shakespeare play in Folger's intimate Elizabethan theater but only a few are allowed entrance to the simulated banquet hall research room and permitted access to the Shakespeare collection. You must first present two references to verify your academic credentials, then fill out a form stating a "serious research objective" for wanting to poke your nose around in the Folger's Elizabethan treasure trove. I did have a serious research objective, just not one I thought Folger's would necessarily approve.

"Briefly, state you research objective:"
(two inches of blank space.)

If I had been honest, I might have written, "I am interested in shedding light on an alterative playwright, on the possibility that someone else wrote all the Shakespeare plays and sonnets." But I abandoned honesty as being foolhardy. I didn't want to lock the door to that treasure trove before it opened, so I simply wrote, " To compare the Shakespeare's plays with other playwrights of his time." It seemed logical to think that if someone other than Shakespeare had written the plays, he or she might have been a contemporary, perhaps another playwright writing under a pseudonym.

In my role as an adjunct professor in Washington College's Graduate Psychology Program on Maryland's Eastern Shore, George Spillish, the department chair, had said, "Sure, I'll write you something." James Siemen, another psychology professor, grinned, shook his head, and added a second recommendation.

I stuffed my request form and supporting documents in a large brown envelope, kissed them goodbye, popped them in the U.S. mail, and waited for my "Welcome to Folgers" letter and my approved research credentials. The wait gave me a little more time to try to digest some of what I had gleaned from the Library of Congress.

I immediately learned that the Shakespeare authorship question stirred more heated controversy than a calmly debated difference of opinion. The Shakespeare supporters – mostly entrenched academicians -- drove their argumental stake in what came to be known as "Fortress Stratford" for the man from Stratford. Other camps – the Jonsonians (Ben Jonson), the Marlins (Christopher Marlow), Baconsonians (Francis Bacon), the Oxfordians (Edward de Vere, the17th Earl of Oxford), circled Fortress Stratford, it's moat filled, its bridge closed, and barrels of hot oil ready to pour from the ramparts. Interlopers were clearly warned to approach at their own risk.

When I surfed the web, I ran across *A Declaration of Reasonable Doubt* -- an online authorship petition. Well-known Shakespearian actors Kenneth Branagh, Derek Jacobi and Mark Rylance were among three-thousand others petitioning for an "open minded academic discussion" of the authorship question. Those who signed were divided as to who might have written the Shakespeare plays, but were of a singular mind on one matter. It wasn't William Shakespeare.

Into the Bowels of the Enemy

My Folger's research credentials arrived late on a Thursday afternoon, too late to drive into D.C. from Annapolis and take full advantage of the day. I was too anxious to wait through the weekend, so I dressed in my "serious academic uniform" – jacket, tie, and fresh haircut – and drove into town early on a Friday morning and found my usual parking spot on South "A" Street.

I hurried the three blocks, skipped up the Folger's steps and tapped Puck's knee as I swung passed him in the vestibule and headed down the long hallway toward the reception desk. I presented my still-fresh credentials to a uniformed guard who compared the laminated photo with my actual face and apparently agreed that the similarity was close enough to warrant a nod. "Report inside," he grunted then glanced back down at a paperback whose pages he had temporarily flattened with his free hand.

I pushed through a heavy paneled door and immediately slid down an Alice In Wonderland rabbit hole, instantly leaving the twenty-first century for a time-warped Elizabethan banquet hall, the elegance and style of which Elizabeth herself would have felt comfortable conducting court-business or cavorting with an endless line of wanna-be suitors smiling and glancing in her direction.

The cross-beamed, three-story ceiling soared above as sunlight winked across the hall from a stained-glass window that dominated the second and third story of the far wall. Two double-tiered candelabras balanced from a huge beam to split the room in thirds while a banister protruded above the first level, hovering over rows of inlaid bookshelves.

At the end, opposite the stained glass window, a narrow canopy floated above a platform that might have held a monarch's throne, yet the space stood oddly empty as I raised my eyes to a replica of Shakespeare's bust which hovered on the wall directly above the platform. After four hundred years, reverence for the man considered a God of literature floated above a fleeting earthly crown.

"How may I assist you," a narrow-chinned woman scowled from behind her desk.

"Shakespeare," I said.

"Of course, Shakespeare. What about him?"

"Well, not exactly Shakespeare, more about his contemporaries. Those around him."

"That's still a lot of territory."

"Yes, I know."

"Miss Ferguson." The woman glanced behind her,

toward a younger woman sitting with her legs crossed. Somewhere in her mid-twenties, the younger woman jumped up as if startled.

"Can you help this gentlemen," the woman said in a tone that suggested more a demand than a request.

"Of course," the younger woman smiled. "Which table would you like?"

"I'm not sure. Somewhere quiet. Where I can spread out."

"Follow me then."

She rounded the desk and led me toward a table at the walled icon's end of the room, the Bard's ghost prepared to glare down and observe my every step or misstep.

"It's a little further back here but I can get those materials to you."

"Get to me how?"

"You tell me what you want, what you're looking for, and I fetch it. I bring it to you."

"Okay."

"So, what are you looking for?"

"I'm not sure."

"Well, that will make it a little hard to find. Where do you want to begin?"

There was something disarming about my guide through this Shakespeare maize. I briefly considered owning up to the truth and making a full confession. Why not? They had opened the door and let me inside. I had my seat and was clinging to it. I didn't think a confession would get me tossed me out, although they could easily refuse to help me if they knew what I was after. "I'm looking for something on Shakespeare's contemporaries," I told her. "Those who wrote in the same style, or close to it."

"That's like asking for Beethoven contemporaries. There are others – Bach, Mozart, contemporaries, but far different styles. Beethoven was Beethoven. There was only one."

Beethoven was Beethoven, I thought. But was Shakespeare Shakespeare?

Over the next several hours, Ellie -- she asked me to call her that – shuffled back-and-forth with arm-loads of briefs, photocopies, clipped articles, and books, some dating back to the turn of the century and few earlier than that. On one delivery, close to noon, she slipped me a folded paper and nodded toward it, walking away as I opened it. "My lunch is in fifteen minutes. Meet me at WE on Pennsylvania. You can buy me lunch."

Pizza and Sacrilege

Just like the Library of Congress, no material left the Folgers, although I had been assigned a locker for over-night holds so that researchers could continue where they left off. I gathered my things and locked up what I was still interested in, then nodded at the "desk boss" -- Ellie had twice called her that -- and left by the theater-end of the building.

Was Ellie flirting with me, I wondered as I headed toward Independence. I was older, but I wouldn't have minded. Maybe tapping Puck's knee had brought me a little luck. I wasn't dating anyone, although I had a strict lower age limit that I was willing to adjust depending on opportunity and circumstance.

I found the WE -- an upscale pizza and sandwich bar with stools stretched along the front the window. I slid onto one and waited. It didn't take long. Ellie must have left early. In less than five minutes, I watched her glance both ways on the other side of Independence then hurry across.

"Not by the window," she said when she burst in, out of breath. "Back in the corner." She nodded toward an empty table then aimed toward it as I followed.

"Have you ordered?" she said as she scooted into a chair.

"Not yet. You wanted me to buy."

"That's why I picked this place. It's quick and cheap. I didn't want you to max out your credit card."

"I'm not all that hungry," I said. "But what can I get for you?"

"I'm not eating."

"Not eating?"

"I'm watching my weight."

"Then there's nothing to get. I'm not hungry either."

"You have to buy something to keep the table. This is their busy time."

"How about a slice of pizza? We can split."

"I could tell you were a big time spender the minute I saw you."

"What else could you tell?"

"More than you know."

****

Ellie's "more than you know" didn't surprise me as I waited in the pizza line. From what I had already learned at the Folger's and at the Library of Congress, it seemed that anyone who had superficially looked into the matter knew more than I.

"How many," the white-capped server looked up and asked as I shuffled forward in line.

"How many?"

"Slices. How many?"

"Just one."

"Small or large?"

"Large."

The Shakespeare authorship controversy had apparently been bubbling under the surface of the literary establishment for well over two centuries. It just hadn't burst through enough for anyone outside the establishment to notice.

"Now that I see it," Ellie said as I carried a slice of pizza back on a paper plate and sat it on the table, "It does look good."

"You want it? It's yours."

"I couldn't eat your half."

"I'll get another one."

"I really couldn't eat a whole one. I'm watching my weight."

"Start with half of this. See if that's enough."

I stood and went to the serving counter, yanked a plastic knife from a tray, strolled back and cut the slice down the center.

"Which half do you want?" she asked.

"You pick."

"The one on the left's a little larger."

"You take that one."

"That would be impolite."

"I insist. Consider it a gift."

"Okay, then. I accept," she said, picking up slightly large half and folding it in half again.

"So what is it," I asked.

"What it what?" She took her first bite and laid the rest back on the plate.

"What is it you know that I don't? Which wouldn't take much."

"Almost any researcher who comes in, who goes to all the trouble to get their credentials, knows more than you… But that's not how I knew." She raised her eyes and glared at me.

"Knew what?"

"That you're a fake. I know what you're up to. I know what you're after."

I waited. Whatever it was she wanted to say, she wanted to say in private. She had asked me to lunch. She didn't need further encouragement.

"That you're the enemy," she said. "You're the wolf in sheep's clothing."

"My research interest is genuine."

"So's the wolf's sniffing around the henhouse."

"How did you know?"

"It was pretty clear from what you had me gather. I'm just an intern but its pretty easy spot a pattern."

"So why didn't you sound the alarm?"

"Now, what would be the fun in that? If you know the wolf's hanging around, wouldn't it more fun to toy with him?"

"Could be a little dangerous. Suppose the wolf turned *you* in for not turning *me* in? There's got to be a rule against interns fraternizing with researchers, sending them clandestine notes, secretly meeting them outside the establishment walls."

"I had a feeling I could trust you. That you wouldn't turn me in."

"Why wouldn't I?"

"Because you could use me. I could help you."

"Why would you want to?"

"Because maybe you're right. Maybe this whole Shakespeare business is nothing but a grand hoax played out on a gullible public, a public who wants to believe that a fine silk can be woven from burlap."

"What do you think, Ellie? Where do you stand?"

"On middle ground. I'm not sure."

"The more I look into it, the more middle ground starts to look a little shaky."

A silence fell as Ellie finished her pizza. "What's your real interest in all his," she asked as she patted her lips with a paper napkin and looked up again.

"More curiosity than anything," I said.

She lowered her chin and raised her eyebrows.

"There's got to be more to it than that."

"I'm a writer. I was looking for a subject when I stumbled onto this."

"Stumbled how?"

"A woman. The usual source of trouble."

"I think I should resent that."

"Do you?"

"Not really."

I explained how I had ruined what was meant to be a romantic weekend in the Maryland Appalachians by studying a pile of alternative-authorship monographs instead of paying attention to the woman who invited me. "She didn't care for that," I said. "She thought my priorities were backward."

"I can't say I blame her," Ellie said.

"Neither can I."

"So she was a skeptic too."

"She thought the evidence for William Shakespeare was scanty at best, that the preponderance of evidence for someone else seemed to be overwhelming. She didn't try to convert me. She simply said, if I wanted to stay naive, that was up to me."

"So now you're trying to advance beyond naiveté?"

"Just trying to see if naive is what it is. But what about you? Why did you get me over here? I assume you don't invite just anyone to buy you a slice of pizza."

"You're the first. Anyway, I'll buy pizza next time."

"So you're saying they'll be a next time? You plan to pay me back? You owe me?"

"How much was it?"

"The pizza? Four ninety five. I got the large. Plus the delivery fee."

"All the way from the counter?"

"I charge by the hour. An hour's my minimum fee."

"Let me ask you a question," she said. "If you like the question, if it points you in a useful direction, will you waive the delivery fee?"

"I'll wave the whole thing. What's the question?"

She leaned forward as if to emphasize the importance of what she was about to say.

"Let me ask you this," she said in a quiet voice. "Thirty-six plays, right? All of them revised several times as they played around the circuit over many years. We have more than one version of Hamlet, for example. No printers or copy machines in those days. All written by hand in quill pen. The director, of course, needed a copy. Each of the players needed one to memorize their lines. And then, with periodic changes, that's lot of copies over a lot of years. Then, added to that, a hundred fifty one sonnets and two major poems. All handwritten. Probably in several drafts."

"Okay."

"So, here's the question. Of all those plays, all those copies, plus any notes the playwright might have written for future plays, all those drafts and notes and any scribbled thoughts for scenes or poems, plus any letters the playwright may have written to anyone about the plays or anything else. Of all that, over all those years, how much do you think survived in the author's own hand?"

I waited. I had no idea.

"It's certainly true," she said. "That many, maybe most, would have been tossed or destroyed over the years. But the plays ran for decades. Quite a few manuscripts remain from lesser poets and playwrights -- Ben Jonson, Christopher Marlow, Philip Massinger, Richard Brome, among others, and obviously from the Queen herself. But from William Shakespeare? The greatest playwright ever. How many do you think? How many total. Notes? Pages? Letters? Anything?"

"You got me."

"Would you believe zero. Nothing. Not a single note. Not one letter, play, part of a play, or scrap of paper that anyone thought worth keeping. Absolutely nothing."

I was stunned. "Nothing?"

"Zero."

"How do you explain that?"

"I don't," she said. "How do *you* explain it? How could it be explained?"

I shrugged.

"Well," she said, leaning back and tightening her lips. "That's not completely true. Not a hundred percent. There is the matter of signatures."

"He signed his name?"

"If you consider a scrawl a signature. And not consistent scrawl at that. Not to any plays. Nothing like that."

"Okay."

"We have six signatures. All on legal documents. Three at the bottom of the three pages of Shakespeare's will. Another was on a court disposition. Then two others related to a mortgage on a gatehouse in the Blackfriars district. All of them are barely legible; all spelled differently and never spelled 'Shakespeare.' More often something closer to 'Shakspere,' as in 'shack.' On one of the will signatures, 'William' is printed as if someone else had written it for him."

"So, you're saying he couldn't write?"

"Not even his own name… And think about it. This is the man who supposedly wrote close to a million of the most beautiful words ever penned in the English language and he couldn't write his name, at least not consistently or legibly.

"Maybe his will signatures were near the end of his life. Maybe his hand shook."

"It shook a lot earlier than that. He couldn't write his name on the earlier documents either.

"Neither of his children could write either. They both signed with an 'X.' Apparently there doesn't seem to be a lot of writing going in that household. And, by the way, there's something else odd about his will. It was several pages long and quite detailed. No books mentioned. No library. Nothing to do with the theater, but what to do with pots and pans. That sort of thing. He willed his second best bed to his wife. Makes you wonder whatever happened to his first best bed."

She glanced at her watch. "Hey, listen. I have to get back. You coming," she asked as she glanced up.

"Obviously I've got a lot more to learn. I'll give you a head start."

"You've only begun to scratch the surface. The

deeper you dig, the murkier it gets."

The Empty Chair

I gave Ellie five minutes, then strolled back and rubbed Puck's knee again as I entered. He had given me luck the first time. He sent Ellie my way. As I rounded the guard desk and passed through the door to the research room, I found another stack waiting on my table.

"The one on top is about David Garrick," Ellie said when she came over and tapped her finger on the cover. "That's his chair over there." She nodded toward a throne-like seat with thick padded armrests shoved back against the wall in the center of a side room. Then she grinned a shy grin, turned and provocatively sashayed back behind the information desk.

I had never heard of David Garrick, although I quickly learned that if it hadn't been for David Garrick – entrepreneur, flamboyant actor, flimflam man, and P.T. Barnum showman -- we may have never heard of William Shakespeare.

By the time Barnum burst onto the stage in the mid-1700's, Shakespeare had been dead a century and a half. Copies of the plays were still around, primarily those from the First Folio printing in 1623, but by Garrick's time the plays themselves had long-since outlived their day. They hadn't been performed for decades. And they may have remained lost to the ages if David Garrick hadn't discovered, or rather rediscovered, Richard III and performed Richard to packed playhouses and rave reviews.

When Garrick rolled into Stratford-Upon-Avon for a performance in the spring of 1769, he quickly convinced the mayor and town counsel that the dramatist -- William Shakespeare -- was born and lived in Stratford and was buried beneath the floor of their tiny church. He persuaded the powers-that- be that money could be made in the name of their hometown son.

Ever the showman, Garrick helped organize the first Stratford-upon-Avon Shakespeare Jubilee -- a three-day, dawn-to-dusk extravaganza that featured clowns and jugglers, a pig-roast, a imported elephant, pony rides for the kids, and round-trip transportation from nearby Oxford and as far away as London.

That first Jubilee's success spawned a second the following year and it wasn't long before little-known William Shakespeare, the same man the town knew as a grain merchant, morphed into William Shakespeare, the revered playwright, and the tiny town of Stratford-Upon-Avon became a Shakespeare shrine and the billion dollar a year tourist industry it is today.

Playing Detective

I drove back to Annapolis in a trance, barely paying attention to the road. By the time I arrived home, Ellie had emailed me.

"Dr. Hutchison. A must read for your search. *This Star of England,* Charlton and Dorothy

Ogburn's 1297 page tome on *William Shakespeare, Man of the Renaissance.* Oh… And by the way, thanks again for that pizza. The whole half slice."

I couldn't quite determine where Ellie fit into all of this. Why would she work for the Folgers, even as an intern, if, as she said, she stood on "middle ground?" And why would she help a psychologist researcher attempt to dig up evidence and stir up controversy for the anti-Folger, anti-Shakespeare side?

I didn't know her well enough to decide, but I did know I liked her. Beyond the fact that she had helped me, her tongue-in-cheek dialogue reminded me of Myrna Loy in Dashiell Hammett's *Thin Man,* and my feeble William Powell-like attempts at snappy retorts.

A Forgotten Earl

The more I sat at my desk in Annapolis and read, the more the accumulating speculation seemed to point down a single path and toward a single individual: Edward de Vere, the 17th Earl of Oxford. De Vere, an aristocrat and nobleman, had long since faded from history's memory until British school teacher J. Thomas Looney (pronounced "Loan…y") became intrigued with the Shakespeare authorship question in 1918 and began his own investigation. Only instead of arguing for one of the usual suspects -- Francis Bacon, Christopher Marlowe, or William Stanley, among others -- Looney plied a new tack.

Rather than examine the candidates, Looney looked to the plays themselves and asked the question: given this particular set of plays, who would the playwright have to be, and what understandings and knowledge would he or she have to possess, in order to write them?

Looney proposed a list of what he called "essential requirements" for authorship which included: someone of recognized genius, known literary credentials, and possessing a classical education, and a wide and intimate knowledge of royalty and royal customs, including royal sports and habits, in addition to a knowledge of law, music, and an in-depth familiarity with Italy and Italian customs, culture, and specific Italian locations.

Several on Looney's list of candidates fit two, three, and sometimes four of his essential requirements but none fit them fit all or even came close. He was about to give up when he happened across the name of Edward de Vere, an obscure and long-forgotten noblemen and intimate of Elizabeth's Court. At a superficial glance, De Vere seemed to meet many on Looney's list, but to Looney's surprise and amazement, on closer examination, Edward de Vere met them all, while William Shakespeare, at least what was known about him, fit none.

Delighted with his discovery, Looney published *Shakespeare Intensified* in 1920, after which Edward de Vere, the 17th Earl of Oxford, was not only included among the list of possible candidates for authorship, but quickly rose to the top of that list.

The Shakespeare Authorship Trust, looking at the authorship question in the same manner many years later, compiled their own list of what they considered essential requirements.

- An extensive knowledge of the law, philosophy, and classical literature.
- An understanding of history, mathematics, and astronomy.
- A detailed knowledge of Elizabethan music, art, horticulture, and heraldry.
- A familiarity with Elizabethan medicine.
- An understanding of military and naval terminology and tactics.
- A thorough acquaintance with the etiquette and manners of the English nobility, including such aristocratic pastimes as falconry, and equestrian and royal sports.
- A comprehensive knowledge of English, French, and Italian court life.

Again, no item on the Trust's list fit the life, education or experience of William Shakespeare. All items on the list, as in Looney's initial investigation, did fit the life, education, and experience of Edward de Vere. If Shakespeare did write the plays, he apparently wrote about everything he knew nothing of – royal life and courtly manners and habits – and nothing of what he did know – the ordinary folk-life in rural England.

The Mystery Man

I rose early the next morning and skipped breakfast, settling instead for a bottomless cup of coffee as I spread a cluster of open books across the kitchen table. By noon, I was tired of endless quagmires and contradictions and needed to get out of the house for a breath of fresh air and gain a fresh perspective. I wedged my MacBook Air into my travel bag and drove down to the Annapolis Harbor. I claimed a corner table on the deck at the Chart House which faced the Annapolis capital dome across the Severn River, the steeple of an 18th century colonial church poking up behind it.

I ordered a Sam Adams and a crabcake sandwich, and stared across the Severn at America's four-hundred-year old history, nothing compared to England's centuries' old history, yet close to the same four-hundred-year period that the author of Shakespeare plays -- whoever he was – traveled around the English countryside, scribbling a new play or revising an old one while preparing to stage an afternoon performance.

George Washington once warmed a seat in McGarvey's Tavern across the river when Annapolis was the capital. But, of course, George apparently sat or slept everywhere. Where did the author of the Shakespeare plays sleep? Where did he hang out? Who were his friends? His enemies? Who was he?

I tried to allow these questions to silently incubate while I ate but my intent evaporated before my crabcake arrived and I dug my AirBook out and shifted around the table to shade the screen from the sun. If Edward de Vere was the actual author, what was known about him? Author or not, I quickly learned that far more was known about him than about William Shakespeare. If de Vere turned out to be the actual playwright, the academicians who so opposed that possibility would suddenly strike a gold mine of information with which to compare the plays and interpret their meaning.

According to Wikipedia, Edward de Vere was born at Castle Hedingham, the family ancestral home in Essex, England on April 12th 1550. When his father, John de Vere, a theater lover and close friend of Queen Elizabeth, died in the summer of 1562, his twelve-year-old son become a ward of the Crown and moved to London under the strict guardianship of William Cecil Burghley, the Queen's private secretary, chief advisor, and later, Lord Treasurer.

Under Cecil's firm hand, Edward followed a rigid daily regime of classic education, including Latin and English literature instruction, French language lessons, cosmography, penmanship, riding, fencing and prayer. Under the demanding eyes of London's best tutors, his regimented days were filled from dawn to dusk, with Sunday's off for church and free time in the afternoon. Arthur Golding, Edward's maternal uncle and literature tutor, was in the midst of translating Ovid's *Metamorphoses* from Latin to English, a translation later recognized as a major influence on the Shakespeare plays.

Building on that classic education, Edward then

matriculated from Cambridge in 1566 and received a degree from Oxford in 1564. He then attended Gray's Inn Law School, known for its student theater productions and for hosting touring theater companies. Gray's also provided the legal education that Looney later listed as one of his prerequisites for the Shakespeare authorship.

By 1571, at the age of twenty-one, Edward was described by a contemporary as "a leading luminary" in Elizabeth's Court and so close to the Queen that, when rumors began to circulate that their relationship was a little too close, a marriage was hastily arranged between the twenty-one-year-old Edward and Anne Cecil, the fifteen-year-old daughter of Edward's wardmaster, Cecil Burghley.

Edward soon escaped his unwelcome marriage for a grand tour of Europe, mostly in Italy, traveling and living in the precise locations that a third of the Shakespeare plays would later take place. Upon his return, he reportedly spoke Italian and dressed so finely that Gabriel Harvey dubbed him "the Italian Earl."

At the same time, Harvey described de Vere as a "prolific" poet "whose countenance shakes spears." Robert Greene dedicated his book, *Card of Fancy* to Edward de Vere, calling him "our preeminent writer." In 1589, author George Puttenham, in his *Art of English Poetry,* added de Vere in his list of eminent English poets, describing him as, "first among us, that noble Gentleman Edward, Earl of Oxford."

Despite such praise, he was apparently not without his faults, not the least of which was living above his means. He was eventually accused of squandering the fortune he inherited on his Italian travels, his extensive wardrobe and lavish lifestyle, and on the elaborate costumes for a string of theater troupes he owned and managed, including the Oxford's Boys, for which he leased of the Blackfriars Theatre, a Globe rival.

Three years after his first wife Anne Cecil, Burghley's daughter, died, Edward married Elizabeth Trentham, one of the Queen's Ladies in Waiting. The newly married couple settled into Brooke House in Hackney, several leagues west of London, where he remained until he died of the plague in 1604 at the age of fifty-four.

In the online record, the Hackney Parish archive specifically indicated that Edward was buried in the Hackney Church on July 6, 1604, although contradicting that report, Edward's first cousin, Percival Golding, later wrote in a family correspondence that, "Edward de Vere, a man in mind and body of absolute accomplishment with honorable endowments, lieth buried at Westminster."

Nineteen years following Edward's death -- with Queen Elizabeth, William Shakespeare, and Edward all long departed -- the first collection of all thirty-seven plays was printed. That First Folio was dedicated to and paid for by Philip Montgomery, the husband of de Vere's youngest daughter Susan, and by William Pembroke, the Earl of Pembroke, a one-time suitor of Edward's elder daughter, Bridget.

Riddle Solved

Some riddles, like a Rubik's Cube, get more complex the more you twist and turn them, and yet there is always an answer buried somewhere in that complication. I had already come across two counter arguments for de Vere as playwright. First that Macbeth, one of the final plays, was written after de Vere died yet well within William Shakespeare's lifetime. It was certainly true that the playwright, whoever he was, weaved magic with words and often evoked ghosts, but scribing beyond the grave seemed an impossible barrier to cross.

In the second counter argument -- also requiring a feat beyond the grave – a shipwreck off Bermuda in the spring of 1609 and widely reported at the time was believed to be the inspiration for the *Tempest* shipwreck even though, by 1609, the only water Edward de Vere could have been aware of would have been the leaks in his coffin.

Stuck again, as I often would be on this twisted journey, I drove back into Washington, presented my credentials at the Folgers' front desk, and found an excuse to get Ellie aside to tell her I had a dozen questions.

"Only a dozen?" she said. "Meet me after work at the Newseum coffee shop on 6th."

****

I slid into a back seat at the only Newseum table available, then stood when I saw Ellie push through the door, stretch her neck, and weave in my direction. "I was wondering how long it would take for you to get back to me," she said as she sat.

"You knew I would?"

"Maybe I was hoping. Hope springs eternal."

"Shakespeare?"

"Alexander Pope."

"You know your authors."

"I ought to. I'm a lit major. That's why I'm working at the Folgers. I need the experience on my resume. There's not much call for lit majors in the real world these days."

"So, why did you major in it?"

"I love it. I always have. Can you think of a better reason?"

"How about practicality?"

"Is that why you write? You're a writer, aren't you? Practicality? Is that your reason?"

"If I got paid by the hour, I'd be well below minimum wage. So what *are* your plans for the future?" I asked.

"You are. You're my plan."

I leaned back and stared. "Me? And exactly how do I fit into your plans? You plan to use me?"

"I was hoping we could use each other. If Shakespeare isn't Shakespeare, and I'm not sure one-way of the other, but if he is and you find proof of that and get published, I'd like to be considered your research assistant. That would look good on my resume. Research is one thing lit majors can do. If they have experience, that is. If there's someone who'll say that I helped them dig up something that matters, I'm all set."

One puzzle solved. I still had no idea what might have motivated a name change on the Shakespeare plays, but at least I knew Ellie's motivation as I stretched my arm across the table to shake hands. My only disappointment, I suppose, was she wasn't interested in me for other reasons. I was considerably older and that would have felt good.

We each ordered coffee and yogurt, the only thing the coffee shop had that passed for food, as we set to work. I wasn't surprised when I glanced up and the room had emptied out two hours later. By then, we had covered a lot of ground, starting with the plays that were supposedly written after Edward de Vere's death.

"Ah, yes," she had said. "The play dates... You know how those dates were determined?"

"I have no idea."

"By a guess, an educated guess, but still a guess. There were no dates of the plays. There were a couple of quartos of individual plays registered by theater owners to protect themselves, but that's just when they were registered, not when they were written."

"Wait a minute. Didn't I see a sequential list of plays and dates somewhere?"

"You certainly did. That's the list that Edmond Malone came up with in 1778, nearly two centuries after de Vere's death and a half-century after David Garrick revived the plays. Malone estimated the dates based on his assumption, a natural one, that William Shakespeare wrote them. After all, his name is on them, so Malone set his dates to fit Shakespeare's presumed working life, from somewhere before 1600 until Shakespeare death in 1616. Ever since then, Malone's presumed dates were the officially accepted play dates used to prove that Shakespeare wrote them and that de Vere couldn't have. The dates didn't fit de Vere's lifetime."

"Backward reasoning."

"It seemed logical if you assumed Shakespeare wrote them."

"What about the historical events? The one's that occurred after de Vere died? The basis for Macbeth and The Tempest?"

"Do you mean the famous shipwreck after de Vere's death -- The Sea Venture, bound with supplies to the Virginia colony, that struck a storm and sank off Bermuda in 1609? De Vere died in 1604. But here's the problem with that. There were dozens of shipwrecks off Bermuda well before 1609 and hundreds afterward. Hundred's more off other islands. But there's an even bigger problem. In the Tempest, the ship hits a storm while sailing from somewhere off North Africa bound for a port in Southern Italy. To crash and sink off Bermuda, the ship would have had to sail completely out of the Mediterranean, past Gibraltar and cross the Atlantic to arrive anywhere near Bermuda in order to wreck off its shores. That would have been months and thousands of miles off course, headed in the wrong direction. That's pretty poor navigating. And add to that the fact that the ship in the Tempest didn't even actually sink. It was scuttled. The characters were swept or crawled ashore in the play."

"I assume you have an explanation for Macbeth too?."

"There is one. In Macbeth, the playwright plays on a theme of equivocation. Which means the use of ambiguous expressions in order to mislead, in Macbeth's case, to mislead the three witches. Equivocation was also famously used by the Gunpowder Plot conspirators to mislead in their trial in 1605, four years after de Vere's death."

"What's the problem with that argument?"

"Nothing. It *was* famously employed in the Gunpowder Plot trial. The problem is, that doesn't help in dating the plays. The concept of equivocation was well known and frequently used long before the Gunpowder Plot trail in 1605. It would have be common knowledge to any playwright and to nearly everyone else. In fact, closer to home, Lord Cecil Burghley, Edward's father-in-law, had written a treatise on the use of equivocation well before the Gunpowder Plot was ever conceived. In addition to that, a Spanish diplomat had written a piece called *The Doctrine of Equivocation* in 1584, translated into English in the early 1590's and widely distributed in England. You would have had to be deaf, dumb and blind not to know of it. I think we can assume the author of the plays was none of those, certainly not dumb."

Ellie watched me shake my head.

"What's *your* problem," she asked. "I can see you have one."

"I'm a psychologist. My problem is motivation. If another name was grafted to the plays, what was the reason? Who did it? Who came up with the idea and why?"

"You want the usual explanation?"

"Let's start with that."

"Social convention. Aristocrats could dabble in plays all they wanted. And often did. As long as their name wasn't attached to their work. Plays were considered beneath them."

She paused to see if that sank in. "The Shakespeare plays were all about the court," she said. "All about Elizabeth's court. As long as they were performed at court there was no problem. At first, it wasn't a problem outside either. Guess what name was on the playbill at the first public performances."

"You tell me."

"Would you believe "Anonymous", quite literally, "Anonymous". Romeo and Juliet by Anonymous. And when a playwright's name finally did appear, it was Shakes-Speare, with a hyphen. Not Shakespeare. That came later when the hyphen was dropped… This might interest you. Edward de Vere was publically known as a shaker of spears for his youthful fencing prowess. If de Vere was the playwright and he needed a pseudonym, for a man of words with double meaning, Shakes-Speare, a shaker of spears, would have suited him perfectly."

"If the name Anonymous was already on the plays, why change it at all? Why not leave it at that?"

She held her napkin up and squashed it with her fist. "If you didn't want to be crushed in those days, you didn't want to cross Cecil Burghley, Edward's wardmaster and father-in-law."

"I don't get it. Why would the plays, whoever wrote them, be of any interest to Burghley?"

"Burghley's prime interest, his only interest, was protecting his queen. And protect her, he did. Anyone who did anything to hint at scandal to the Queen's reputation could easily find his severed head staked at the end of the old London Bridge. Many did. There was a constant flow of blood dripping from those stakes."

"What did that have to do with plays?"

"It had everything to do with the plays. The plays were all about the Court. All about royal life. Even the staunch Shakespeare supporters admit that Polonius in Hamlet is a direct parody of Burghley right down to his speech patterns. What they don't say is how William Shakespeare, a commoner, could have had any contact with Burghley, let alone mock his speech.

A Missing Piece

On my drive back to Annapolis, something bothered me about that conversation but I couldn't put my finger on it. I still couldn't when I woke that night and staggered into the kitchen at 3 A.M., brewed a cup of coffee and sat at the table with a notebook and a pencil and listed names and dates with a few notes.

- Cecil Burghley, the Queen Elizabeth's chief minister and henchman, died in 1598. Edward de Vere died in 1604.
- The Queen died in 1603.
- William Shakespeare died in 1616.
- By the time the First Folio was printed in 1623, they were all dead. De Vere, the Queen, Burghley.

If Ellie was right, and the whole point to hiding the real author's name was to protect Edward de Vere's aristocratic reputation, then why protect that reputation after he died? Protect it from whom? Anyone who mattered, who would have cared, was already dead.

I emailed Ellie, asked her to Skype me later, and went back to bed, still unable to sleep. When my iPhone beeped me awake at six-thirty, I reached across the bed, picked it up and read. "If you're up early. Skype me at seven."

At a quarter of seven, I was up at the kitchen table again, a cup of coffee steaming next to me, ready to Skype.

"Good morning," she said when she appeared onscreen. "You look bright and cheery for this time of day."

"You better clean your screen."

"What couldn't wait? Why didn't you just come in to town?"

"The dates, the First Folio date, why not put a false name on the plays at that point? Whoever had them printed must have known who wrote them. And everyone who mattered was dead, right?"

"Not quite everyone. Don't forget who paid for them, who had them published -- the husband of Susan de Vere, Edward's youngest daughter. She certainly would have known if her father had written them. Maybe that's why she had them printed. She knew they would soon be out of fashion and that they might be lost forever."

"Wouldn't that have been the perfect time to set the record straight? To get her father's name on them?"

"Not as easy as you might think. Keep in mind; there were no publishers in those days. No bookstores. No Amazon. Not that many people read and the few books that were available were expensive. It you had a book you wanted to get out, you went down to a printer and gave him a handwritten copy. Handwritten copies are all there were before they were printed and bound. When your order was ready, you came back down to pick them up, paid what you owed and carted them off. Plays were like movie scripts today. People went to see plays. They didn't buy scripts. Someone wanted them printed regardless."

"Susan."

"The plays weren't being staged any longer. If Susan hadn't had them printed, Shakespeare, or whoever the playwright was, might have been a minor figure today. We might have had a few plays, but not a full collection of all thirty-seven."

"You said not quite everyone who mattered was dead."

"Elizabeth was dead. That was true. But her replacement, James I, had every reason to care. His very throne was at stake.

The Tutor Rose

With a penchant for drama herself, Ellie said she to had dress for work, leaving me with questions still dangling in cyberspace. As usual, she tossed me a clue, a name -- Elisabeth 'Betty' Sears – that pointed me in a new direction.

When I Googled Betty Sears, I found her short book entitled *Shakespeare and The Tudor Rose* online. I skimmed it on my Kindle and then sat back and read it in detail. When I finished, I stepped out on my sundeck and stared out at a cloudless sky, hoping that blank canvas might help organize the jumbled pieces into some recognizable form.

Of course, I thought as I considered Betty Sears conjecture. I'm a clinical psychologist. Why hadn't I considered it before? After all, Elizabeth was a relatively young woman when she unexpectedly ascended to the throne at the age of twenty-five. She was always noted for her energy and playfulness. She was athletic by nature. She could ride with the best of men and often outran them. As queen, she threw lavish banquets, sometimes disappearing into her private quarters with a male courtier for hours then suddenly reappearing with a grin on her face. One famous painting shows her on her toes, dancing with her dress raised above her ankles as she cavorted with her longtime paramour, Robert Dudley, the Earl of Leicester.

This beautiful, fun loving, energetic Queen with her glorious red hair and men bowing and scraping at her feet, was able to command anything she wanted. Are we really to believe that she was a virgin, that she never had sex with anyone her entire life? And, if she did have sex, how did she protect herself? How did she keep from getting pregnant?

It was Betty Sears' contention, based on a reasoned argument and a considerable array of documented facts, that the "Virgin Queen" was not a virgin at all, that she did indeed have sex, and that she bore a child and perhaps more than one. The child in whom Sears took particular interest was, in Sears's view, the son of the Queen and her favorite poet and courtier, Edward de Vere, the 17th Earl of Oxford.

According to Sears, the timing and opportunity meshed perfectly. The Queen and de Vere spent a good deal of documented time together in the late summer and early fall of 1573. In May of the following year, just as the she was about to embark on her long-planned summer visits around her realm, she abruptly interrupted preparations, dismissed all but the royal physician and a few trusted servants, and retired with de Vere to Havering-on-Bowre, one of de Vere's many private estates. The Queen remained at Havering until early July, long after the progress was scheduled to begin, then suddenly reappeared without explanation and carried on as abruptly as she left.

The resulting child, according to Sears, was placed in the care of Mary Browne, one of the Queen's ladies-in-waiting who had lost her own infant son the previous October. The child, mothered by Browne, married to Henry Wriothesley, the second Earl of

Southampton, grew up at the Wriothesley manor in Titchfield near Southampton, was thus slated to inherit the title of Henry Wriothesley, the *third* Earl of Southampton. Elizabeth, in the meantime, remained a "provisional virgin" for marital purposes, still allegedly capable of producing a first-born heir to the throne.

I slid my laptop further back on the table to allow room to breath and keep my mind from whirling. The Virgin Queen *not* a virgin? She *bore* a child? That would clearly have been scandalous, but enough to shake or break a nation?

The Fine Art and Loss of Politics

Gordon Alexander, a Washington College professor of history and an English literature fanatic weighed in at close to three hundred pounds. His stature filled half his tiny office while his psychological presence overwhelmed a conference room at least as much as his bulk. Every year or so he toyed with the possibility of bariatric surgery but, at the last minute, always opted out in favor of a liquid diet of protein powder and prune juice until he lost ten pounds before slowly regaining it and rethinking the procedure.

"How's it going," I asked as I slid in across from Alex in Washington College's faculty dining.

"You see any prune juice in front of me?"

"Too early to rethink the procedure," I asked.

"I haven't gained an ounce since you last saw me."

"How do you know that?"

"I guess. I don't look down. I feel lighter."

"Speaking of the lack of evidence, and maybe denial, that's why I wanted to see you."

I brought him up to date on my interest in the Shakespeare authorship and on Betty Sear's theory on the birth of a son. He grinned and shook his head, then plopped his huge elbows on the table and leaned across as if he were about to devour me. "Every time we shoot one of their horses down," he boomed, "they trot another one out from their stable."

"Another playwright?"

"Another *possible* playwright. How many are there? Six? Seven? A dozen?"

"Edward de Vere among them."

"Some think the Queen wrote the plays. Rubbish. Utter rubbish."

"I take it that the whole idea of an alterative playwright is not popular among the academic elite."

"Let me put it this way. A young rising professor advocating that someone else wrote the Shakespeare plays is not advancing his career."

"I can imagine."

"Can you imagine what it might be like to be a tenured professor, maybe at Oxford or Cambridge, near the end of your career, having built that career on writing the ten volume definitive history of William Shakespeare and then finding out that someone else wrote the plays, that William was a grand hoax?"

"I can see how that might get someone's ire up. What's your opinion on the matter?"

"The play's the thing. What difference does it

make?"

"For a psychologist it might make a great deal of difference. All creativity comes from someone. Knowing who that someone is tells a lot about what he created. Knowing who Van Gogh was, what his life was like, and how he suffered, adds a tremendous understanding to the meaning of his paintings. If you know where they came from, you know what they mean."

Alex leaned back, his chair disappearing somewhere behind him. "Did you come here to debate? If you have, you won't get one from me."

"I came to pick your brain. Not on the literature side. On the history side. Elizabethan history. The Queen's virginity."

"You just can't seem to avoid controversy."

"It's a magnet. It draws me."

"Sometimes what draws you can draw you over the edge... What is it you wish to know?"

"The simplest question. *Was* she a virgin?"

"Who knows? She always claimed to be. She always said she was married to England, not that she didn't occasionally consider marriage. She came close to being betrothed to the Duke of Anjou, the son of Henry II of France. She called him her 'frog.' He looked like a frog. And then there was Robert Dudley, the Earl of Leicester. The problem with Leicester, he was already inconveniently married. And when his wife died under mysterious circumstances -- she fell down a short flight of stairs and broke her neck -- Elizabeth's subjects were rightly suspicious and would have none of Leicester."

"So she never married."

"She couldn't. Her entire foreign policy rested to her supposed virginity. She had inherited a lot of land from her father. A string of castles. A number of useless monasteries. But not much else. Her father, Henry VIII, had bled the county dry building and refurbishing his own castles, not to mention his wasteful French military campaign. Elizabeth had no standing army and certainly no navy. What money she did have came from uncertain taxes, most of that from Londoners, who increasingly wanted to keep it for themselves."

"So, she had…?"

"She had herself. She had her wit. Her cunning. She had her beauty. She was a handsome woman and she knew it. Everyone knew it. She knew it and took advantage of it."

"For?

"Diplomacy. The European powers coveted her tiny island. They hungered for it. They salivated. Particularly France and Spain. They each wanted free access to the channel and to keep the other out. They each wanted to merge with England against the other. To merge through marriage. A first son born of Elizabeth and a prince or a duke of either France or Spain could produce a common heir to rule both thrones."

"Power politics."

"Today, it's money. Then, and for a long time after, it was alliances. Alliances through marriage. By the end of the reigns of most European royalty a century and a half later, they were all second and third cousins."

"Royal incest.

"Pretty close. And Elizabeth played that game with the same cunning she applied to her chess. She secretly promised to marry them all. When the French ambassador arrived, she shunted him aside and whispered that she truly planned to marry his guy but that the ambassador for Spain was due in the fall with his own marital hopes. She urged patience on the French, telling the French ambassador she wanted to let the Spanish down as easily as possible."

"And, of course, she told the Spanish the same damn thing."

"A brilliant strategy and one that worked well. It kept both counties, both bitter enemies, at bay for years. If Elizabeth had married either one, the other would have immediately swept across the channel and attacked. Spain finally caught onto her ruse when she became too old to produce an heir. Phillip, having grown uneasy on his Spanish throne, sent the largest and most powerful armada ever assembled with orders to attack. And they should have won. Everyone expected they would. Elizabeth gave a famous speech to that effect at Tilbury."

"Why didn't they?"

"The English ships were fewer in number, but far smaller and lightly armed, so they were nimble and quick. They took less draft. They could easily sail close to shore and do ends around the Spanish Armada."

"A huge dog after an agile rabbit."

"And then there was Raleigh, Elizabeth's experienced strategist commanding her ragtag fleet.

"Sir Walter Raleigh."

"After several days of a fruitless chase, the Spaniards put into Calais and dropped anchor to restock and recuperate. On a moonless night, while the Spaniards slept, Raleigh loaded a staggered line of longboats with dried hay, lit them on fire on an incoming tide and set them adrift. At first all there was were scattered fires slowly drifting across the water. Then one Spanish vessel caught, then another. Then a gunpowder room was breached and flames exploded in a dozen directions at once, lighting the decks of galleons in a haphazard pattern.

"Chaos and mayhem ensued. Shouts and screams drifted across the harbor. Men on fire dove and swam among the flames. A few vessels attempted to raise sail and flee, careening off hulls and slamming into one another. By first light of day, with black smoke still billowing from charred shells, a few had actually managed to slip from the inferno, many of those severely damaged. What was left of the once invincible fleet limped up the channel and around the tip of Scotland, skirting rocky shoals in stormy weather. Less than a third that sailed out managed to stagger back. Suddenly, and unexpectedly, tiny England commanded the seas. Elizabeth, by putting the inevitable off, by promising marriage, had won."

"That's quite a story."

"A story of unfathomable twists and turns. History is full of them. If we could predict them, they wouldn't be a surprise."

"History as told by the victors. But what do the victors hold back in telling their story? What don't I yet know?

The Passage of Time

After lunch with Alex, I ambled over to the Washington College Counseling Center to visit friends then drove back to Annapolis just as the sun was setting. That had always been a quiet, peaceful time -- a break from teaching and counseling as I drifted home under a golden-red sky.

Just before I hit Rt. 50, I spotted a herd of deer quietly standing along the line of trees beyond an open field. I often stopped when I saw them there. Somehow, they reminded me of the passage of time, every year a different group, a different configuration. The only thing constant was me, and I was always that much older every time I stopped and looked.

All the Elizabethan characters that now danced through my mind had once stood among the fields somewhere in England, they too, perhaps, contemplating their fate and the passage of time. And now, four hundred years later, I was standing alone, staring across an open field. What secrets did my predecessors hold? What confidences did they carry with them to the grave? What clues did they leave behind that could be pieced together to reveal those secrets?

Some of the pieces of the puzzle had already begun to fit. A pattern had begun to emerge. Cecil Burghley, the Queen's chief advisor, henchman, and protector was Edward de Vere's father-in-law. He must have been aware of de Vere's reputation as an acclaimed. He knew that his

son-in-law was a playwright who managed his own
company of players, although no plays were ever found in
de Vere's his own name.

At the same time de Vere managed his theatrical
company, the Shakespeare plays were being performed
under the name "Anonymous," the credits later changed to
"Shakes-Spear."

If the plays were all about the Elizabethan court, as
alleged, and if de Vere was the Queen's lover and father of
their clandestine child, would Burghley not have
considered it his sworn duty to protect the realm and his
queen by distancing the playwright and father from
Elizabeth and her court? According to Gordon Alexander,
Elizabeth's entire foreign policy rested on her not having a
child, on remaining virgin material to produce a future
heir. If she already had a child, particularly one by a
prominent English earl, the ascendency would be settled.
She would have been of no marital value and England
would have been open to immediate attack.

Some of that made sense. At least, there was
coherence to it. But why William Shakespeare? If there
was a conspiracy of concealment, what part did he play in
that? Where did he fit into the puzzle?

Armed with more information, which always
seemed to lead to more questions than answers, it was time
for another Skype chat with Ellie.

The Opportunity and the Opportunist

"The right time and the right place," Ellie said,

smiling at me on my computer screen. "Timing is everything."

"There was a William Shakespeare, right? He wasn't a creation?"

"He very much existed. There was no need to create him."

"Who was he? What do we know about him?"

"Very little if you assume he wasn't the author of the plays."

"How much is 'very little.'"

"Ten. That's the number. Ten documented facts. That's it. That's all there is. And that's from hundreds of investigators looking into it, trying to uncover more, for over a hundred years."

"What are they?"

"The facts? Hold on. I have a list here somewhere. I'll look them up."

She disappeared from view and popped up again in less than a minute. "Okay. You're not going to believe this. Hang on. I'll email them."

She looked down and typed. When I heard a 'bing,' I opened my email and brought up a list:

THE DOCUMENTED LIFE OF WILLIAM SHAXPERE

1) William Shaxpere baptized in Stratford on April 26, 1564.
2) The Worcester register records a marriage license to Willelmum Shaxpere and Anna

Whateley of Temple Grafton. William was eighteen. Anne was twenty-six and three months pregnant.

3) A dwelling, New Place in Stratford, is reconveyed to William Shakspere.

4) William Shakspere is named in the King's Remembrance Subsidy Roll as a tax defaulter in Bishopsgate ward. He is recorded as "among those either dead, departed or gone out of the ward." A second record indicated that he had moved across the river to Sussex.

5) In a list of Stratford grain hoarders, William Shakspere is identified as having illegally held 80 bushels corn during a shortage.

6) A lease is signed for the Globe Theatre between the landowner Sir Nicholas Brend, the Burbage brothers and five members of the Lord Chamberlain's company, which included Shakspere.

7) William Shexpere is by apothecary Philip Rogers, seeking to recover the unpaid balance on a sale of twenty bushels of malt.

8) Three Nearly Illegible Will Signatures.

9) The burial register of Trinity Church Stratford records the burial of 'Will Shakspere gent.' What is believed to be his gravestone on the floor of he church does not bear his name. It is thought that his

grave lies between that of his wife Anne and his daughter Susanna.

Ellie waited for me to study the list and glance up. "Well, what do you think of it," she asked.

"That's it?"

"That's all that can be definitively traced to William Shakspere, the man from Stratford. There are other mentions of a Shakespeare, the author of the plays, but there's no way to know if the two are the same."

"Okay," I said. "If that's all there is, how can volumes be written about Shakespeare?"

"Easy. Here's how you do it. You start with the assumption that the William of Stratford was the playwright. It's a natural assumption. His name is on them, well at least a close approximation of his name. After David Garrick revived the forgotten plays in the mid-1700's, a century and a half after they were written, everyone initially thought Shakespeare did write them. Garrick thought so. Why wouldn't he?"

"Even if he did, that's still not much to go on. Not much to write about. Not from that list."

"You don't need much if you assume that William Shakespeare was the actual author."

"Enlighten me."

"There's a respected Cambridge expert who has written what he calls the Shakespeare's definitive history in ten thick volumes."

"That's a lot of words. How's he do it?

"He adds a telling tag to his title. Instead of *The History of William Shakespeare,* his complete title is *The Compete History of William Shakespeare and His Times.* That leaves him a lot of room to maneuver. Volume two in the leather bound set is titled *Shakespeare's Education.* The problem there is, there is no record of Shakespeare's education. He may have attended school in Stratford. There may have been a small county school there, but no records of who attended. If you're writing about Shakespeare's education, you simply say that he 'may' have attended or 'probably' attended."

"So you're saying there were gaps. That this so called expert filled them in."

"It's mostly fill. He would start with something like, 'We know Shakespeare grew up in Stratford. They probably had a school there, at least for the lower grades. From the records that do exist from other county schools in other towns, this is what he would have studied.' You get it? The whole volume is not about Shakespeare's education. It's about England's 16th century educational system and what it might have been like for Shakespeare. After all, we know he was a playwright and a master of words, so he must have learned something somewhere. You start with an imagined school he 'probably' or 'may have' attended."

"Even so. Even if there was a primary school, how much could he have learned at a county school?"

"There's another problem. Records from all the elite universities do exist. Cambridge. Oxford. The one's de Vere attended for which there is a record. There is no record there for a William Shakespeare or a William Shakspere. Yet the playwright, whoever he was, was well versed in Latin as well as English history, the law, and medicine, not to mention royal habits, customs, and pastimes."

"So how does the expert deal with that gap?"

"He ignores it. When pressed, he says the budding playwright hung around the pubs on the London docks. A lot of foreign sailors hung out there. He picked it up what he knew in bits and pieces."

"At a bar?"

"Apparently alcohol loosens the mind to spill all it knows and absorb all it hears."

"And to think I wasted all that time in school," I said.

"It's the same sorth of stretch in Volume II in *The Complete History of William Shakespeare and His Times* - the theater volume. Again, there's far more about 'his times," than about 'The Compete History of William Shakespeare.' A couple a paragraphs would have taken care of that. But there *was* lot to write about the Elizabethan theater, more than enough to fill a volume. But just not Shakespeare's part in it."

Ellie waited while I absorbed what she was saying.

"Okay," I said. " We know that plays were being presented under Anonymous to start. Then William Shakespeare's name suddenly appears on them."

"Shake-Speare, not Shakespeare. At least not at

first."

"What's your theory about that? Why the change from Anonymous to Shake whatever?"

"There's one thing we do know from Shakespeare's documented record. In 1597, at the age of thirty-three, he came into enough money to return to his Stratford and buy New Place, the second largest house in town. What do you think of that," Ellie asked, raising an eyebrow.

"I don't know what to think."

"There wasn't that much money to be made in the theater, at least not early on. Suddenly, he comes into cash. A lot of cash."

"Hush money?"

"I think he was paid to use his name. And paid a 'goodly sum,' as they said in those days. And I think those payments continued. There was an odd stipulation in Elizabeth Trentham's will, de Vere's second wife. She bequeathed a 'goodly sum' to someone she identified only as 'my dumb man", the payments to continue for the remainder of his life. There's no indication of who that might have been. Trentham died in 1612. Shakespeare died in 1616, four years later. Just like today, dumb could mean deaf and dumb, or it could mean just plain dumb."

"William Shakespeare."

"Doesn't say. Could be."

The Proof

Ellie's theory was simple. Like Betty Sears, she contended that de Vere had an affair with Queen Elizabeth that resulted in a clandestine son, a potential heir to the throne and a huge problem for English diplomacy. Cecil Burghley, the Queen's guardian and protector, demanded the playwright and father distance himself from court and the Queen. His plays about the court where already being performed in public under "Anonymous." Another personage was suddenly mandatory to obfuscate the trail. Someone from far out in the countryside. Someone with no connection to the Queen or the court. Someone no one ever heard of.

William Shakspere, a theater hanger-on at the time, just happened to have the perfect name for a man of words and innuendo, for a man already known as a "shaker of spears." Mr. Shakspere was paid a goodly sum -- a continuing goodly some -- to use his name. He applied the initial payment to the purchase of the second best house in his small town of Stratford. A century and a half later, when David Garrick revived the long forgotten plays, everyone, including Garrick, assumed that Shakespeare wrote them. The academics took up the mantle, built their case around it, then dug their heals in to defend their ground.

Even though the preponderance of evidence favored de Vere as playwright, it was still all circumstantial – a classic education that fit the language and content of the plays, an intimate knowledge of the court and court habits and Italian travels to the precise locations where a third of the plays took place. But that's all the evidence there was. Circumstantial. Where was the solid proof, the smoking gun? Or, in the case of the plays, where was a single note or a manuscript in playwright's own handwriting, whoever he was?

And then, added a' top that pile of circumstance, the person who paid for the publication of the First Folio just happened to be Edward de Vere's youngest daughter, Susan Vere. It must have been Susan, or someone on her behalf, who carried the original handwritten copies down to the printer for printing.

Trying to sift through all this and make sense of it, one question kept reoccurring. What happened to those original handwritten manuscripts? When the printer finished his printing and Susan went down to pick up what she had paid for, what did she answer when the printer sat her father's originals on the counter and asked, "What do you want me to do with these? Toss them? Burn them?"

What would Susan have answered after going to all the trouble and expense to preserve her father's love and labor? And, if she did carry those originals back with those first folios, what did she do with them? Might she have hidden them, hoping that later generations would discover them to prove her father's authorship? If she did hide them, were they destroyed or lost over the centuries or are they buried somewhere? And, if so, where?

Why, after all these years, no matter who wrote the plays, has nothing turned up in the playwright's own handwriting? That conclusive proof, if it exists, still awaits discovery.

A Door Squeaks Partially Open

At this point in my convoluted journey of discovery, I was satisfied that I had uncovered all the facts I could. At least for the moment, there was nothing left to find. I had a plausible theory but no way to prove it. It was still all speculation. There was no undeniable evidence resting solidly in one camp or the other. I had gone as far as I could. I had reached a dead-end.

I settled back into my normal routine – private practice therapy, teaching a graduate psychology class, and counseling at Washington College. Not surprisingly, the ghost of Edward de Vere continued to haunt me, pleading to make his cause right, much as Hamlet's ghost had. But what could I do? There was nowhere else to turn. Or, so I thought.

As often happens to writers, or anyone else with an unsolved problem, I awoke in the middle of the night with a possible answer floating in my head. The boy, I thought, he alleged son of the Queen and Edward de Vere. What about the boy?

The more I thought about it, the less aristocratic embarrassment struck me as a plausible motivation for a name change. From a psychologist's perspective, it didn't have the solid ring of truth. It felt weak. Particularly following de Vere's death. Why would embarrassment still apply post-mortem? On the other hand, a clandestine child that threatened the imminent invasion of England rang a whole lot of bells, maybe enough to shake an Elizabethan tower until it toppled.

According to Ellie, the alleged son's identity was known -- Henry Wriothesley, 3rd Earl of Southampton. She had said that the 2nd Earl of Southampton and his wife, Mary Brown, one of the Queen's ladies in waiting, had raised Wriothesley.

What happened to the boy's body after his death? Where was he buried? Could his body be found and exhumed? Could DNA evidence be brought to bear on the authorship question? Could it be definitively proven that Henry Wriothesley was, in fact, the son of the "Virgin Queen" and Edward de Vere? That wouldn't prove de Vere's authorship, but it would certainly show an intimate connection between de Vere and Queen, and a formidable incentive for distancing the playwright from anything to do with Elizabeth and her court.

I crawled out of bed and staggered into the kitchen. I started coffee brewing, flipped open my MacBook and Googled Henry Wriothesley, 3rd Earl of Southampton.

Halfway down the second paragraph, I stiffened and leaned in closer to read the words again. As one of James I[st] first official acts on his way down from Scotland to accept the crown, he had ordered Henry Wriothesley to the Tower on unspecified charges. Did James have information about the boy that could threaten his ascension to the throne?

Reading further down, Wriothesley had been

released in less than a fortnight and nothing further came of it. Might James have had knowledge of the clandestine child between Edward de Vere and his immediate predecessor? But would the fact that the son was illegitimate have mattered? Elizabeth herself was illegitimate, declared so by her own father.

Did James or one of his emissaries trot over to the Tower and have a little chat with Wriothesley? Might Wriothesley have said he wanted no part of the throne, that he had been around it all his life, and understood and reviled the constant turmoil his mother had faced?

Whatever happened to gain Wriothesley's release, he remained James' loyal subject and devoted the rest of his life in the service of his new king.

I put my MacBook to sleep and left the house in the dark. I needed the cool night air to wake me up and settle my thinking. By the time I'd circled the block and returned home, I knew where I was headed. I knew what I needed to do.

Forensics

For a DNA test, I needed a body. For a DNA match, I needed two. If Henry Wriothesley was the son of de Vere and the Queen, Wriothesley's DNA should match both his mother's and his father's. But that particular match was a non-starter. Even if I could locate and dig up de Vere's body and get a viable sample, there was no way I could exhume the Queen's body, permanently entombed in her private chamber in Westminster Abby. Even if I could substantiate Edward de Vere as Wriothesley's father, that might implicate the Queen but it would in no way prove the Queen was Wriothesley's mother.

Still, sometimes a crack opens in what seems like a locked door and widens on closer inspection.

****

"Myocardial DNA," Myra Bainbridge, a Washington College biology professor responded when I sat in her office and described my dilemma. "You don't need DNA from the Queen. Myocardial DNA, a particular kind, passes from the mother down to all her children, but only her daughters can pass it on the next generation. It only passes down the generations through the female line. You get it? You understand what I'm saying?"

"I think so. You're saying I don't need the Queen's body. I can skip one generation back. I need the Queen's mother."

"You'll have no luck with that either. I understand that Anne Boleyn is pretty well chopped up and encased under an unmarked slab less than sixty-five yard from where she was beheaded."

"Then Boleyn's mother. Or ...."

"Exactly. Any mother's mother or grandmother's grandmother as far back as you can identify one and have her exhumed. Check it out. You'll see."

****

I did check it out with the "old bones" DNA expert at the University of Pennsylvania who emailed me back that a viable DNA sample could be analyzed as back as far as Elizabeth's time and that it could very well prove parentage against another sample. But to accomplish that, of course, I would also need a sample from Wriothesley's body – the expert recommended a wisdom tooth – to match against a female ancestor somewhere back along Elizabeth's maternal line. If her grandmother's or one of her great grandmother's myocardial DNA matched Wriothesley's then the last mother along that line – Elizabeth -- was Wriothesley's mother.

But all that would prove was that the Queen was hardly a virgin, that she had at least one child, and that child was Henry Wriothesley. It would prove that there had to be father, but not *which* father. To establish Edward de Vere as Wriothesley's father, I would need a sample from either de Vere's body of from de Vere's mother's since all his mother's DNA, myocardial or otherwise, would pass to Edward and that DNA would pass on to Edward's son.

But first things first, I thought. Edward de Vere, supposedly the Queen's lover, father of her child, and possible playwright. Still, even if I were able locate de Vere's body, what sort of permission would I need to exhume it and extract a sample? Would that even be allowed?

To start with, conflicting documents pointed to two burial locations -- difficult unless de Vere's body, like

Anne Boleyn's, was chopped up and separated. The online Hackney church records indicated that Edward de Vere died of the plague in 1604 and was buried in Hackney's St Augustine's church on July 6th. To substantiate that, De Vere's second wife, Elizabeth Trentham -- who outlived her husband by eight years -- stipulated in her will that she "wished to be buried in the Church at Hackney as near upon the body of my said late dear and noble lord and husband Edward as may be possible."

Pretty clear. Except, a conflict exists. Despite all that documented evidence, several years after Edward's and Trentham's death and burial, Percival Golding, Edward's younger cousin who knew his uncle well, explicitly stated in a surviving family document that, "Edward de Vere, 17th Earl of Oxford, a man in mind and body absolutely accomplished with honorable endowments, died at his house at Hackney in the month of June 1604 and lieth buried at Westminster."

Oddly, and unusual according to what I found about the established precedent, a man of de Vere's status and accomplishments left no will to distribute his worldly possession or indicate his burial wishes, at least no will that survived, although his wife did leave a will. Furthermore, a burial in Westminster Abbey would have been more appropriate for an earl of de Vere's stature.

With a little further research, I discovered an illustration and description of the huge Vere family tomb jutting into the aisle of St. John the Baptist's chapel in the North Transept of Westminster Abbey. Edward's uncle Francis Vere's tomb was shown there, his armor atop a canopy above him. Horace Vere, Edward's cousin lay next to Francis, and Henry Vere, the only son of Edward and the inheritor of the title 18th Earl of Oxford, was next to Henry. But not Henry's father, not Edward de Vere, the 17th Earl, at least none listed in the online in the Westminster burial records, although the graphic of the monument did depict a stone at the foot of the Vere tomb with the inscribed words, "Body Buried Beneath."

So where was Edward de Vere's body, in the Hackney churchyard or beneath the floor of Westminster Abby? Was he buried in one place and then moved to another? How could Percival Golding, a member of the family who knew his uncle Edward well, make such a glaring mistake in a family document? And if Edward was buried in Westminster or moved there later, why is there no record of that?

In The Air and On the Ground

With all these questions swirling, I knew what I had to do. Spring break was coming up at Washington College in less than a month, which meant three weeks off from teaching and counseling. I was far enough into this pursuit, why not follow it through and see where it led? Why not travel to England, skulk around in a few castles, catacombs, and graveyards and stir up a little ancient dust among that scattered debris?

I had a light therapy load, so I rescheduled my regular clients and told my secretary to leave that time-block free. When I contacted the Westminster

Archives Office, they emailed back that two academic references would grant me access to their 15th century burial records. I used the same two references that gained me access to the Folgers, then purchased my ticket and packed my bag.

Faded Names and Dates

I might have changed my mind if I had waited. A trip to a local graveyard led to much discouragement. Bill Tubman, a friend and my boss at the time, asked me the obvious when I told him of my plans.

"So," Bill said over lunch. "Let me see if I have this straight. This guy your are looking for could be buried in Westminster Abbey but there's no record of that, right?"

"I want to take a closer look at that, but, right, no record online that I can find."

"And if he turns out to buried in a churchyard… That would that have been when?"

"1604."

"And you think he might still be there?"

"Westminster or Hackney. He's got to be somewhere."

"Finish your lunch. I want to show you something."

I grabbed my sandwich, rode with Bill through the countryside back-roads of Kent County, Maryland, and just finished eating as Bill pulled into the shaded parking lot of St. Paul's Episcopal Church.

"Follow me," he said, as we got out and he led me through a gate and along a path that ran through St. Paul's graveyard. "Over here," he said, taking a few more steps and stopping in front of a grave. "You know who that is," he asked, nodding toward the tombstone.

"Somebody dead."

"The best known dead in the yard. That's Tallula Bankhead, a famous movie star in the thirties and forties. She owned a farm near here. She called it her plantation. This is where she wanted to be buried."

"What's a whisky bottle doing where flowers ought to be?"

"She still has admirers. She once said she had only two vices, booze and men and she preferred to indulge them together."

"Why did you bring me here?"

"Look at those dates."

"1902 to1968."

"Easy to read, right? Now, follow me." He led me farther up the hill. "These are the oldest graves along here," he said, ambling along a back row. "Most of them dating back to the early1700's, right after the church was built when Kent Island was still a Maryland Colony."

It started to dawn me what he was getting at.

"How many of these can you read," he asked. "Names and dates?"

Without even bending closer, the answer was obvious.

"What's the date for your guy even if he is somewhere in that churchyard?"

"1604."

"That's a lot of wind and rain over a lot of years - A

lot of wear and tear. I'd be very surprised if you'd find the tombstone "

But I had my ticket. I had scheduled time off. It was settled. I was going.

****

"Upstairs in back," Kashif Mahla, my bearded, Pakistani B&B innkeeper informed me. "Down the corridor. It's quiet back there and quite comfortable. Breakfast is at eight-thirty. Would that be good for you?"

I assured him it would, then climbed the stairs, tossed my suitcase on a stand and flopped on a soft mattress, waiting for Maryland time to catch up with London time.

I had booked the B&B for ten days in the Harrow-on-Hill section of outer London, a thirty-five minute train ride to the Thames and the center of town. I had hoped ten days would allow enough time for the first stop of my adventure. There were other places I needed to visit.

"What carries you here," Kashif asked when I came down for breakfast the next morning. "Business or pleasure?"

"Investigation," I said as Kashif served the standard English breakfast – two eggs sunny-side up flanked by two slices of broiled tomato, a thick grilled sausage and a hefty scoop of dark baked beans with a plate of toast on the side.

Kashif stiffened and stepped back. "Investigation? I charge a fixed price," he said. "I assure you, I always pay my…"

"Nothing like that," I said, looking up. "I'm a psychologist. It's a historical investigation."

"Ahh…" His chest lifted again as he turned and reached for a pot of tea to sit in front of me.

Before long I was spilling the whole authorship story to two other guests who ambled down and joined us -- all ears and full of questions. I informed them that I was off to Westminster Abbey this morning to examine four century-old burial records.

"Don't leave without letting us know what you discover," an impeccably dressed Scot said, his wife nodding agreement as she spread jam on her toast and clinked her knife on the plate.

Underground

Margaret Chase Whatley, Chief Curator for Westminster Abbey's Ancient Records and Archives Division, had scheduled me for 10 A.M. sharp with the admonishment, "Please be on time. Your research will be limited to one hour."

I arrived at the Westminster's underground station at nine thirty, crossed Bridge Street and proceeded to the west side of the building as the Abbey's huge spires shaded a morning sun that traced across the Thames at a bend in the river. A narrow door, four steps down with a posted block-letter "301," gave no hint of the treasure trove that lay behind its formidable barrier – eight centuries of documents, parchments and records stretching back to early medieval times.

I pressed the buzzer and waited for a click as the heavy door jerked partially open and I shoved through.

A stone-walled cavern greeted me as I entered, widening as I stepped further in. I had an eerie sense that I was following the ancient footsteps of depraved heretics and condemned witches awaiting a ritual beheading at the end of the line. Maybe not, I thought to calm myself. Maybe the trail to a monk's wine cellar, storing ancient bottles for ceremonial or medicinal purposes, or perhaps to induce a deeper meditative state during long hours of wear-and-tear on prayerful knees.

"Dr. Hutchison," a heavy-tanned, mid-twenties desk-jockey asked as she lifted her arm and glanced at her watch. "You're five minutes early. Have a seat." She eyed a row of hardback chairs strung out to the door. In exactly three minutes by my watch, a tall, slender woman with a tightly curled twist in her dark hair pushed through a swinging side door and stuck her hand out as she approached. "Right on time," she said. "Good to see you. I'm Madeline Bruning, an assistant curator. Any photo equipment on you?"

"My iPhone."

"Please leave that with Sherry." She nodded toward the desk- jockey who had slid an empty plastic tray across her desk. "Also," she added, "if you have any ink or any sort of writing instruments place them here. Do you have a notebook and paper?"

I slid out a three ring binder from my shoulder bag.

"Leave the bag. You can keep the notepad. And one #2 pencil, which we'll provide... Also, if you don't mind." She nodded toward a box of skin-colored, latex gloves and asked me to slip on a pair and follow her through the same door she had entered.

A single row of desks ran down a central aisle of a much smaller room with alcoves of stacked manuscripts and documents extending evenly along both sides.

"The depth of these walls holds the temperature even," the assistant curator said, catching me glancing at them. "It's good for preservation... I understand you want to examine our ancient burial records."

"In the period from around 1600 and maybe up to thirty years later."

"For those, I'm afraid I'm required to remain with you and turn the pages. As you can imagine, they're extremely fragile. We may get around to digitizing them. Other projects stand first in line however... Wait here."

She slipped on her own pair of gloves, then disappeared and returned with a huge, hard-covered account book -- grayed on its binder and yellowed around its edges. She laid it gingerly in front of me and delicately opened to a page she had marked with a thin leather strip. "Be careful not to touch. You cannot run your finger down the columns. Just keep a distance."

The ancient book before me - three inches thick on either side as it lay exposed – overwhelmed a third of the small table. The assistant curator hovered close enough over my shoulder to breath hot breath on my neck as I stared down at names and dates quill-penned four-hundred years earlier, their fine lined entries scribed in a precise, legible script as if the scriber knew his work might be reviewed and judged centuries later. The entries – the names and dates of burials and their cathedral locations – ran from 1598 on the top left of the ledger to1604 at the bottom on the right, the same year Edward de Vere was reportedly buried in the Hackney Churchyard.

I leaned as close as I could without breathing directly on the parchment, fearing I might scatter several pages in a sudden puff of dust and fragments. I didn't expect to find Edward de Vere on the page in front of me or on the next as I glanced up and nodded for my overseer to turned it over. I assumed that other researchers had trod this path before and if de Vere had left his shadowed mark it would have been discovered long ago. Instead, I was looking for some sort of odd or uneven spacing or some kind of overwriting that might have obliterated what it covered.

"Try this," the assistant curator said. Sensing the sort of detail I was searching for, she handed me a rectangular magnifying glass. Still, magnified or naked-eyed, nothing suspicious emerged on any of the pages I had already examined and looked for any relevant entries through 1624, the year de Vere's cousin wrote to family members that his uncle was buried at Westminster. If de Vere was in Westminster and the family knew of it, it apparently went unrecorded, an unlikely event considering the Abbey's obsessive record keeping.

"Any possibility of a burial not recorded," I glanced up and asked.

"Lot's of those early on. But only one that we are aware of beyond 1505 and that one was deliberate -- the grave of the unknown soldier from World War I. If you tell me more of what you're looking for, perhaps I can help."

I shrugged and decided to level with her. I told here I was looking for someone who was allegedly buried in the Hackney churchyard whose cousin later said he wasn't there at all, that he was buried in Westminster.

"Highly doubtful," the assistant curator said. "But let me put this away and check on something. I'll be back."

She gently closed the book and carried it off, then returned a few minutes later and sat across from me. "I did find something that might be of interest. Not exactly what you're looking for but related."

"I appreciate your help."

"You mentioned Hackney. I looked that up. There was a body removed from the Hackney church and reburied in Westminster around those dates you were looking at."

"That is interesting."

"That one is recorded though. That's how I could find it."

"Who was it?"

"A Margaret Douglas, Countess of Lennox. She was reinterred in the Abbey in 1603, twenty-one years after her death and her recorded burial in Hackney."

"Wouldn't that be unusual? To move a body?"

"Extremely. But this order came from high up."

"From?"

"From King James. Margaret Douglas was his

grandmother. After he ascended to the throne, he had her body removed from Hackney and reinterred here in Westminster. Does that help?"

"I'm not sure, but it might. Thank you."

Since my allocated hour was nearly up and there was nothing else I wanted to see, I thanked my helper and left with a little more information than I'd carried in, but no existing record of Edward de Vere and apparently no de Vere body.

When I checked my iPhone as I crossed the plaza toward the Thames, I found an email from Ellie. "How did your Westminster adventure go? Skype me when you get a chance. Oh, and by the way, have lunch at Salieri's on the Strand. I'll explain later."

If I calculated right, 10 AM London time made it 5 AM on the East Coast. If I tried to catch Ellie after work, say at six in the evening, that would make it eleven at night in London. With jetlag still hanging over me and with everything I still had to do, I wasn't sure I'd still be sitting up straight by eleven, but I did want to talk to her. I already had a number of questions.

In The Temple

Westminster Abby's heavy, double-door visitor's entrance swung open at ten. I had found no archival record of an Edward de Vere's burial in Westminster's archives, but there were records of de Vere bodies interred in a family tomb in the St. John Evangelist Chapel in

Westminster's North Tempest. While I was there, why not take a look?

By the time I arrived at the front of the Abbey, a line of blue-uniformed schoolgirls were filing in behind a robust woman leading her flock with the wave of a red school flag. I waited as the group clustered inside before snaking around them and raising my eyes to the magnificence of man's creativity for the glory of God. The cathedral's vaulted ceiling, soaring five stories above, spread narrowing waves of golden spires that drew my eyes toward the center of the polished tile dome and forced me to lean back against a marble pillar to hold my balance.

As soon as my equilibrium stabilized, I focused straight ahead on a gleaming golden cross that beckoned me forward. I clicked my heels across the tiled floor, turned left at the central sanctuary and slipped into the North Tempest. I stopped and turned sharply to squarely come face-to-face what I'd come to see. A life size effigy of the battle hero Sir Francis Vere, Edward de Vere's uncle, lay prone on a black marble slab, his full suit of armor spread out above him on an open canopy supported by four kneeling knights. If the monument was meant to impress, it did.

A stone etched on the floor marked the final resting place of Edward de Vere's only son, the 18th Earl. And next to him, lay Horace Vere, Edward's cousin. And at my feet, as I glanced straight down, was a stone simply marked, "Body Buried Beneath." But, who's body? Could it be Edward de Vere, secretly laid to rest and never officially recorded? Obviously, room remained beneath that floor in 1604. Edward's son was somehow later wedged in there in 1625, twenty-four years after his father's death. Was his father already there, awaiting his son?

No definitive answers lay in front of me, and none were housed in the archive either. But since I was in the cathedral anyway, I took the opportunity to join the line that circled Queen Elizabeth's white marble effigy in the tiny Lady Chapel just around the corner from the Vere's. Whether the Queen's earthly remains lay encased inside in the chest high monument or buried beneath my feet, whatever secrets she held would remain forever lost and sealed.

I crossed to the South Tempest and ambled past Poet's Corner -- the resting places of Chaucer, Ben Jonson, Charles Dickens, and a high-walled effigy of William Shakespeare leaning his right elbow on a stack of books with his name and dates of birth and death etched beneath and the words, "Buried in Stratford Upon Avon." That struck me as odd in a way I hadn't considered before. With all the other well-known authors of their era buried in Westminster, why not the most famous one of all? If Shakespeare's contemporaries knew who he was, why wasn't he interred in Poet's Corner along side the rest? Yet, another unanswered question. Another mystery.

By the time I left the cathedral and re-entered London's sunlight and traffic, it was close to noon and I was hungry. "Have lunch at Salieri's on the Strand," Ellie had emailed. She said she would explain. I planned to Skype her later anyway. If I hadn't eaten there, I knew I'd hear about it.

When I Googled Salieri's on my iPhone, I found it was a good walk and although I could have hailed a cab, I thought the walk would hasten my remaining adjustment to British time while a noon meal might induce my digestive system to comply.

****

Salieri's -- a good half-mile down the Strand toward the old London gate – served up an eclectic mix of pasta, grilled fish, and marinated steak. I ordered spaghetti Neapolitan with a glass of Chianti and looked around for any sort of clue to indicate why Ellie had wanted me to eat there, but found none. The pasta arrived al dente and mildly spiced, but the atmosphere was pure American-movie Italian – half-round Neapolitan style cushioned booths, beads and bobbles dangling from red side curtains, and stenciled frescos around the walls and across the ceiling. I left with my stomach satisfied far more than my curiosity.

****

"What time is it over there," Ellie asked when her face popped up on my computer screen that evening.

"Let's just say it's late and leave it at that. It's dark."

"How was your day? How did it go?"

"Nothing ventured, nothing gained. Or in my case, a lot of time and effort ventured with not much gained."

"How about Westminster? Nothing there?"

"Nothing in the archives. I looked at the scribe's handwriting the entries appeared authentic. Nothing suspicious."

"Not necessarily."

"What do you mean? I was there."

"Nothing in the archives. But that doesn't necessarily mean no body."

"Wait a minute," I said, having only a vague idea what she was implying. "Are you saying they buried de Vere but didn't keep a record of it?"

"Apparently Percival Golding, Edward's cousin, thought so. Or else he was terribly mistaken."

"What do you know that you're not telling me?"

"More speculation than knowledge."

"Speculate."

"Edward de Vere should have been buried in Westminster. It would have been proper protocol for an earl of his rank and stature. After all, his son was buried there."

"I saw that."

"If the son, why not the father? Why wasn't Edward?"

"You tell me. Why not?"

"That's the problem. Accurate Westminster burial records *were* protocol. Name. Internment date. Cathedral location. You saw them."

"I was blurry eyed by the time I was done."

"There is only one way that standard procedure could have been overridden... Well, two ways, actually.

There are only two who could have done that."

"I'm all ears."

"The Archbishop of Canterbury, the head of the church could have ordered it. And then the only one above him."

"James," I blurted. "The king."

"Exactly. Which would have been James, the same monarch, who, with censorship still tight and sedition still rampant among distraught Catholics, would also have had to approve all publications. That would have included the First Folio. James would have benefited from another name on the plays if he knew that the actual playwright and the former queen produced a child who might topple his throne."

"But how would any of that connect with a Westminster burial. Or the lack of one."

"Maybe that was part of James' deal with Susan Vere, Edward's daughter. Maybe she was forced to accept a name change in order to obtain permission to publish the plays. In return, James might have allowed her father's burial in the family tomb in Westminster with the caveat no name, no record."

"What about the mention of a Hackney burial in de Vere's second wife's will?"

"Maybe de Vere was originally buried in Hackney and moved later."

"Wait a minute," I said, starting to fit the pieces together. "The archives did have a record of a body moved from Hackney to Westminster which was ordered by James. He had his grandmother moved. If he did it once, maybe he did it again, but secretly this time. Maybe de Vere was recorded as buried in Hackney but that burial never took place. Maybe he was immediately buried in Westminster."

"That's a lot of maybies."

"This whole convoluted mess is riddled with holes and supposition. By the way, that restaurant you sent me to, Salieri's on the Strand, What was that all about?"

"A walkable distance from Westminster, right?"

"A long walk"

"If you had kept walking, it would have been about the same from there to London's old gate. Salieri's is halfway between?"

"Why is that important?"

"You were eating on the site of the greatest power broker in his day. Salieri's is the former location of Cecil House, the palatial residence of the most powerful individual in England beyond the Queen herself. Cecil House positioned Cecil Burghley exactly in the center between London's new money and commerce to the west, and the power of the throne to the east, the perfect vantage point to observe and manipulate both. And, guess what? It's the same house in which Edward de Vere was raised after he was sent there as Burghley's ward. It's where he would have had frequent and easy contact with the Queen and were he met Burghley's daughter Anne, who Burghley later forced him to marry."

"Burghley's name seems to come up a lot."

"As the Queen's protector and Edward's father-in-law, nothing passed his eyes or ears unnoticed.

Whatever happened, Burghley was either at the center of it or knew about it. Find Burghley's part in all this and you've found the key."

I thanked Ellie and said good might. I told her I would keep her informed on what I was up to and that I was certain I would have a lot more questions as I weaved my way through this Elizabethan maze.

London

I awoke from my first sound night's sleep since I arrived and brought the inn-keeper and his guests up to date at the breakfast table before taking the train into town for a visit to the Museum of London. I wanted to get a better idea of what London was like in de Vere's day.

For all its ancient history, the Museum of London itself makes an ultra-modern statement of glass and polished metal backed up against what remains of the old walled city in the Aldersgate section of London.

As I headed up the steps and through the door, I thought of what Ellie had said about Cecil Burghley; that he would either have been at the center of any intrigue or the driving force behind it. That notion reminded me of another question Ellie had asked. She had been discussing the fact that the First Folio was dedicated to and paid for by the husband of Susan Vere, Edward's youngest daughter. I recalled Ellie asking what I thought Susan would have done with her father's handwritten originals. Did I think she would have tossed them? And if Susan didn't destroy them, what did she do with them? Is undeniable handwritten proof of who actually wrote the plays still hidden or buried somewhere? If so, where?

I had come to the London Museum to dig through several layers of the ancient city's history. Based on Ellie's leading questions, there was also a more specific site I wanted to investigate -- Cecil House, Burghley's London residence. Ellie had said that Burghley had positioned himself directly in the center of power, between London's money and commerce on one side and the Queen's royal power on the other. To drive her point home, she had me sitting and eating pasta in what might have been the center of Burghley's entrance hall.

As I headed toward the Elizabethan History Room, I spotted an open door further down marked "Research" and stepped in that direction. I slipped into a chair in a middle bank of computers, typed in Cecil Burghley, and studied my first hit.

- William Cecil Burghley
- Born: September 13, 1520
- Died: August 4, 1598
- English statesman and chief advisor of Queen Elizabeth I
- Secretary of State and Lord High Treasurer

Further down, it read, "Lord William Cecil Burghley, born in Stamford in 1520, served as Queen Elizabeth I chief advisor for most of her reign. He was twice Secretary of State (1550–1553 and 1558–1572) and Lord High Treasurer from 1572 until his death. From 1558 on, Cecil Burghley remained a constant presence in Elizabeth's court and at her side. No significant matter escaped his attention and most were shaped under his power and influence."

Further down again it read, "Burghley established a far-reaching espionage network and kept detailed accounts of all matters related to the court and his household."

I glanced up from the computer screen, trying to sift through what I had just read, then looked down and reread the exact words. *"Kept detailed accounts of all matters related to the court and his household."*

Edward de Vere was clearly an integral part of that household. He grew up there as Burghley's ward. He married Burghley's daughter. If the Shakespeare plays were, in fact, all about court, Burghley would surely have known the playwright, whoever it was. It seemed generally accepted, even among staunch Shakespeare supporters, that Burghley himself was buffooned and lambasted as Polonius in Hamlet. How could Burghley not have known who had penned disparaging words against him personally? How could he not have known who had made a fool of him onstage? And who could have gotten away with that?

It suddenly occurred to me, that if Burghley had kept an exacting account of everything, including everyone and everything in his household, he would certainly have kept a record of any seditious plays written by his son-in-law. He may have even kept an original copy, or at least a mention of one or more by the playwright stashed somewhere. I wondered what might have happened to Burghley's pile of spy books and accounts. Over his long career, there must have been hundreds of them, maybe thousands. What clues or silver bullets might they conceal?

I had had enough conjecture and speculation for the moment. I needed something physical to focus on, something beyond dispute. I pushed my chair back, retraced my steps down the main museum hall and wandered into the Elizabethan Room.

At the room's center as, a ten-by-ten meter model of 15th century London spread out in front of me, the facsimile stretching beyond the old walled city to include the Whitehall royal complex and Westminster. And right between the two, central on the Strand just as Ellie had indicated, stood Cecil House, Burghley's palatial estate and gardens. From its' twin towers, England's chief spy could keep an eye out for trouble in either direction. Anything that passed back-and-forth would have to pass directly in front of his door. The details were described on an interactive map. Touch a structure and discover its history.

Lord Cecil Burghley constructed Cecil House on the north side of the Strand, directly across from the Savoy, in 1560. The 'L' shaped brick residence stood three stories high with twin turret towers supporting each corner and a central bay extending over an entrance that opened to a wide inner court. The twenty acres behind the residence incorporate a paved tennis court, a bowling alley, and a formal English garden and orchard.

Upon Burghley's death in 1598, Cecil House became the official residence of Burghley's eldest son Robert Cecil, Earl of

Exeter, and was thus renamed Exeter House.
Converted in 1676 into an Exeter Exchange
of offices suites, the building was
demolished in the spring of 1829.

The full London replica included Southwark, the
sinful, raucous playground across the Thames with it's
cock-fights, bear-bating, gambling, pickpockets, flimflam
artists and, of course, the newly established theaters – the
Swan, the Bankside and the Globe.

The other prominent feature of the 16th century
model was the original London Bridge – a compact city in
itself -- that spanned the Thames to connect the city with
Southwark and the only means of crossing the river other
than rowing or hailing a water taxi. Over two hundred
shops, apartments, living quarters and other assorted
structures were crammed together on the massive span.
Some buildings rose seven stories and jutted over water
rushing beneath their bay windows. A mid-bridge chapel
faced a central park. Homes, shops and stalls spread out in
both directions -- a butcher, a baker, a candlestick maker, a
blacksmith, a leather binder, a tailor, sewers and
seamstress, a wig shop, a miller grinding his daily grind on
a watermill. All manner of carriages, wagons, two and four
wheeled pushcarts, horses, goats, sheep, pigs and cattle
were driven by leather-pants herders swinging sticks,
whips, and sharp tongues as they squeezed in and around a
constantly moving array of mixed and assorted riders,
traders, thieves and pedestrians nudging and rubbing
elbows and nerves as they jostled for hoof and shoulder

space.

After six hundred years of stalwart service and the opulence, the bridge's subsequent replacement was a highly efficient, four-lane, bump-in-the-road -- nothing to speak of or even notice modern span.

Fire

One other exhibit drew me further down the hall – a smaller, lighted replica of 1666 London, a city ablaze. Bursting flames lit the model's sky as if a miniature God had stretched a burning finger down to avenge the city for some awful transgression. Fire and heat licked the slats of wooden buildings and passed their devastation down the line as if each was kindling for the next. The inferno gutted the city inside the old Roman wall, then extended west toward Whitehall, pulling back and stopping only after consuming 70,000 homes, eating away at St. Pauls' roof and ravaging the infrastructure of nearly every city administrative building. When the flames died, old inner city no longer existed.

As I leaned in closer, it appeared that whatever structure had replaced the original Cecil House along the Strand had been threatened but spared. Anything that may have remained stored or hidden there from Cecil's days, either by him or one of his heirs, might have remained for awhile, buried in those cellars or walls until the building was ripped from its foundation and crushed into rubble nearly two centuries after that devastating fire.

****

I slept late the next day and missed my B&B breakfast. The inn-keeper wasn't there and neither were any of this other guests, but he left an open tin of crumpets on the table an electric teapot with a note, "Help yourself."

With no particular plan for the day, I spent the morning digging a little deeper into de Vere's character – finding an apparent conglomeration of virtues, warts, and scandals. In one letter to Burghley while on his travels in Italy, de Vere accused his wife, Burghley's daughter, of "cuckolding" him. She had apparently produced a child he couldn't have fathered since he was in Europe at the time the telling deed was done. When he returned, he refused to live with her and setup household in Fisher's Folly, a small estate outside Bishop's Gate just to the north of the city. It stood directly across from the old Bedlam Insane Asylum and close to the original location of the Globe Theater before it was later dismantled board-by-board in a rental dispute and carted off to Southwark.

I had a ticket the following night for Hamlet and decided to use the day to follow de Vere's trail, since de Vere's ghost, much like Hamlet's, seemed to be following me. I took the train back into town, got off at Liverpool Station, and walked two blocks south and a block west at what was once Bishop's Gate. Nothing but a plaque remained, tacked to a church appropriately named "Church of St. Bishopsgate."

I stood with the church door to my left and faced

north. I held forward a printout of old London, stepped passed where Bishopsgate once stood, then counted buildings and paced off distances until I reached New Street with Rose Alley just beyond. If my calculations were right, this would be the original location of Fisher's Folly. In its place stood a row of three story brick buildings with a smaller concrete structure poking its nose out half way down Rose Alley, which turned out to be a dress shop called "Therapy" with a "50% Off Sale" in the window. That seemed fitting. De Vere was reportedly a clotheshorse and after his exorbitant tailoring expenses in Italy, he could have used 50% off.

As I stood there, trying to imagine what Fisher's Folly must have been like four hundred years earlier, the brevity of a single lifetime struck me as well as the coincidence of who we are and the time we are born. I was standing close to the spot where de Vere might have walked for exercise after a hardy meal. If the time and place of my birth wasn't off, I could have nodded as he passed and asked how his day had gone, or if he had started a new play based on his recent Italian travels.

Now, four centuries later, all I could do was speculate on what the occupant of Fisher's Folly might have thought as he passed through the gate to his newly acquired residence. Did he sort through his new Italian wardrobe or did he immediately sit down at his desk and grab his quill to write? If de Vere's ghost had followed me to Fisher's Folly and was watching over my shoulder, he remained silent, perhaps with an enigmatic grin stretched across his face.

****

The original location of the Globe – the first theater built after de Vere's return and a short walk from Fisher's Folly – was equally disappointing. Instead of that three-story, first-of-its-kind, thatched roof structure, a laudromat and a row of modest shops lowered their awning windows in shame, as if realizing they were no match for the history and glory they replaced.

Since my timing was off again and my carriage and driver weren't waiting outside on a 16th century opening night, I walked to the underground station under my own steam and rode back to Harrow-on-Hill as we swept up hoards of London commuters along the way.

The Globe

The anticipation of a night at the theater excited me. I had tickets for Hamlet, the play that allegedly paralleled Edward de Vere's life. Just as Hamlet lived in the strictly ordered household of Polonius, an admitted parody of Cecil Burghley, de Vere was reared in Burghley's strictly ordered household. Just as Hamlet was torn in his engagement to Polonius' daughter, Ophelia, de Vere was torn in his engagement to Burghley's daughter Anne. Hamlet wrote a play within a play. De Vere was a recognized playwright who managed his own theater company. Just as Hamlet accidentally stabbed and killed

Polonius for spying on him, de Vere, as an adolescent, stabbed and killed an undercook that Burghley had sent to spy on him. Just as Hamlet abandoned his home for an extended stay abroad before returning home to his troubles, de Vere left England for an extended stay in Italy before retuning home to his troubles.

Was this a lot of parallels or a lot of coincidences? If it is true that writers write of themselves, maybe "parallels" was the answer.

****

A current Globe, a hundred yards west of the original, gently rose in front of me as my cab crossed the new, bump-in-the-road, London Bridge and a setting sun stretched its long shadows across the theater. I had doubled the price of standing up in the yard -- a tomato-tossing distance in the old days -- for a cushioned seat in the second tier.

After arriving early for the seven-thirty performance, I tipped the cabby, crossed in front of the theater and headed up the steps of the Swan Bar and Restaurant to sip a slow beer. I slid into a window seat with the Globe's timbered white-plaster to my left and an expansive view of the Thames and a darkening city across the river. It was going to be a good evening.

****

The theater filled quickly, with many of the open-air

yarders carrying an umbrella to lean on when their knees began to buckle or to raise quickly in a downpour. A stage canopy protected the performers from inclement weather and a thatched-roof overhang sheltered the cushioned seats. But tonight, as on hundreds of Elizabethan nights, the show must and would go on, full moon or downpour.

At close to seven-thirty, Bernardo, a castle watchman, entered stage-right. He immediately heard footsteps in the dark and cried out, "Who's there?" Before Bernardo could shake off his fear, two other guards joined him telling him they had seen the ghost of their recently departed King and feared his apparition might reappear to haunt them. Horatio, terrified when he entered after witnessing the ghost, believed that Hamlet's father may have returned from the grave with a message for his son. Horatio sets out to inform Hamlet of what he has seen.

The play proceeded quickly -- the audience enraptured by the play's intensity, the yarders leaning forward as one, only jostling and stretching at intermission. No barbs or tomatoes were thrown. The modern yarders held their emotions in better check than raucous 15th century theatergoers who usually imbibed a bit before a performance. They would have spent much of the afternoon losing money on a cockfight or satisfying a baser need with one of Southwark's ladies-in-waiting.

In the final scene of the final act, violence erupted, leaving the audience drawing a collective breath. Swords, knives, and poison cups mistakenly switch hands until, one after the other, all on stage succumbed to death. Hamlet, near his own death, lay in the arms of his best friend and companion Horatio as he spoke his final plea.

> "O good Horatio, what a wounded name,
> Things standing thus unknown,
> Shall live behind me!
> If thou didst ever hold me in thy heart
> And in this harsh world
> Draw thy breath in pain to tell my story."

As Hamlet drew his final breath and slumped, a deadly silence hovered over the audience. Then a crescendo of applause slowly rose as the cast clasped hands, held their arms in the air and stepped to the lip of the stage, all smiles and glances. They knew they had transported us back to another time and place. For a brief two-and-a-half hours, we had lived in Hamlet's skin, felt his anguish, wallowed in his indecision and, in the end, grieved his death. We found ourselves lost in the story and had to shake ourselves back into the twenty-first century.

As I walked across Artist Bridge to escape the theater crowd and catch a cab on the other side, Hamlet's dying words to his best friend Horatio still reverberated. Had I just heard the words of Edward de Vere spoken through Hamlet? Hamlet had pleaded to Horatio to remember Hamlet's wounded name and tell his story. Were these Edward de Vere's words to tell his story and his request to restore his wounded name upon his death?

****

On the following day, I opened my MacBook to reread the scene in which Hamlet and Horatio run across a pair of gravediggers, when Hamlet lifts the skull, holds it directly in front of his face, stares squarely in those empty eye sockets, and says to Horatio, "Alas Horatio, I knew him. A fine fellow of infinite jest," then speaks these words directly to the skull:

> And now where be your gibes?
> Your gambols? Your songs?
> Your flashes of merriment?
> Not one to mock your grinning
> Quite fallen chap.

I stared out my B&B window at second story rooftops across the way. I had started this journey to see if there might be a means to determine which fallen chap the author might be. Was it William Shakespeare or Edward de Vere whose words Hamlet spoke? Was the true author's name removed to distance him and his plays and from a queen with whom he had a child?

A practical question, and one that spurred my journey: would DNA from that child, Henry Wriothesley, match either the Queen's or de Vere's? Would Wriothesley's DNA match both? Would that match powerfully suggest a motivation for a name change?

That question led to one more task in London. DNA required bodies. Much like Hamlet having eyed a skull and asked what happened to that poor fellow, it was time dig up some old graves, examine their scrapings through the eye of an electron microscope and remark to those old bones, "At last, poor fellow. Who are you? Now we finally know."

Hackney

The once tranquil, stream-and-pasture village of Hackney now found itself choked inside London's congested traffic as the Underground system I rode rose above-ground and dropped me off on a two story wooden platform that rattled its complaints before the train squeaked its doors shut and sped off again. I had seen a print of the 17th century village before those tracks butcher knifed their way through empty wheat fields and cut across winding country lanes.

As a writer and a dreamer – perhaps they're the same – I wanted that quiet village to remain just as idyllic as it appeared in the print. It's not that I mind change. I just wanted change at my own discretion. But as I clunked down those wooden stairs and stepped onto concrete, the honking of horns and clatter of traffic rudely assured me that my timing was off again. As usual, I was four hundred years too late. Instead of waiting for the clamping of hooves and the whirl of carriage wheels to pass in front me, I stood with the rest of a gathering crowd for the blinking "Don't Walk" sign to change before we hurried to avoid the next rush of cars, cabs and buses.

I crossed Mare Street and stood on the corner of Mare and Lower Chapton for a good view up Chapton. I held up two maps, one of old Hackney and one of the new, comparing both with a photograph of Hackney's original St. Augustine Church in whose yard Edward de Vere was reportedly buried. When I looked uphill on Chapton, toward the Brooke House in which Edward de Vere spent his final days with his second wife, Elizabeth Trentham, I could barely see its outline in the distance. Still, it was there. I had found it.

****

To avoid the sort of disappointment I felt for the loss of the pristine village, or at least to delay it, halfway up the hill toward Brooke House I stepped inside Hana's Coffee Shop, slid into a booth, and spread my maps and printouts in front of a steaming cup of coffee.

I didn't expect Brook House to be as I imagined it, or anything near what it was when de Vere lived there, but as I left the coffee shop and circled the Brook House I found that a gigantic, cereal box like structure stood in place of the once-expansive, multi-leveled opulent home.

In it's place stood a second Brook House -- the Brook House Sixth Form College. It seems the Nazi blitz had swooped over the original estate and struck its first blow in the spring of 1940, followed by a second and a third before the wrecking ball finished the job in 1955. The destruction and reconstruction was complete. The Brook House Sixth Form College, with its long hallways and rows of classrooms stood in place of frescoed staterooms, elegant parlors, and thick-pillowed boudoirs once meant to pamper the tastes and desires of aristocrats and royalty.

All that I had left to envision of that 16th century architectural masterpiece was my own imagination as I skirted the south side of the Sixth Form College and walked along the edge of a parking lot that paved over a once blooming garden of marigolds, hyacinth, lilies, and an orchard of ripening apples and pears. As I turned and walked back downhill, I carried with me a heavy sense of sadness and loss.

Up Against the Wall

When I reached the bottom of Mare Street and approached what remained of the original Hackney Church, its massive stone tower rose triumphantly in what would have been the center of the old village. But the tower was all that remained of that once proud structure. An empty grass covered lawn filled the space behind the tower, where the original church once stood.

"May I assist you," a black-frocked priest hurried across the lawn and asked.

"I'm not sure," I said. "I'm looking for a body somewhere back here."

"You're likely standing on one," he said, stretching out a black-shoed toe and tapping the grass.

"Where are the gravestones? The markers?"

"They're all over there," he said, nodding across the lawn. "Stacked in piles against the wall."

"How did that happen?"

"They were moved."

"Why?"

"No one knows., but likely when they tore the old church down. They wanted to clear space for trees and a park. No one could read them by then anyway. The names and dates, all of it, long washed away."

"So there's no idea who they were? Who was buried here?"

"We know exactly who they were, just not where they are. There's a registry. Who exactly are you looking for?"

"A 16th century earl. Reportedly buried here in 1604."

"An earl... he may be over there. In one of those raised boxes closer to the church. But none of those can be read either... If you don't mind my asking, might you have an interest in attending Sunday service in the new church?"

"I probably won't be here on Sunday."

"Rather ironic, isn't it? They tore the old church down when the congregation grew too large to hold more than a thousand parishioners. The new church was built to hold five thousand. Less than a hundred attend now. I preach to tired nods and empty space. If you change your mind you'd be welcome."

"The registry," I asked. "You said there was a registry. Where can I find it?"

"In the archives. At the library."

After the priest seemed to satisfy his curiosity and wander off, I walked across the wide lawn to the wall that bordered the south side of the property and examined row-after-row of stacked tombstones layered three and four deep, each flattened, pot-marked, and eroded. Scattered gray dots and indentations were all that remained of the names and dates once etched on their surfaces. If Edward de Vere was one of those depressions, even if his name had survived centuries of wind and weather, there would be no way to tell where his marker might have stood before someone yanked it up, dragged it across the lawn and stacked it against the wall. If de Vere's body was somewhere on this churchyard, it was lost to the ages. There was no way to find it.

Archival Resurrection

Word-of-mouth is not the same as eye-on-paper. I had known that there was a documented record of de Vere's burial in Westminster through this cousin's family journal. If, as the Hackney priest had indicated, there was an archival record of de Vere's burial in the Hackney, why not have a look?

"You're not the first," the librarian said. "I can't show you the original document. It's too fragile, but photocopy though. Have a seat."

I plunked down at a thick-legged table among rows of stacked nonfiction and watched the librarian disappear and return with a folder containing a columned list of sequential names and dates. "Halfway down on the right," she said as she laid it in front of me.

I ran my finger down the column.

Name: Edward de Vere, 17 Earl of Oxford

Born: 12 Apr 1550, Castle Hedingham, Essex, England
Died: 24 Jun 1604, Brook House, Hackney, Middlesex.
Buried: 6 Jul 1604, in Hackney Church, Middlesex

The record was clear. De Vere was recorded as buried in Hackney. But whether or not that body was actually there, or ever was there, was still open to question.

I stood up to return the folder when the librarian wandered back with an empathetic grin. "Here," she said, laying a black-and-white photograph of a body-size box in front of me. "Did you notice that the record states *in* the church, not in the *churchyard?*"

I looked up at her.

"Makes all the difference, doesn't it," she said. "Have you read what someone has written beneath the box?"

I glanced down again at a neat, curled handwriting beneath the photo.

Believed to be the burial bench of Edward de Vere,
17th Earl of Oxford standing along the back,
south-side wall of the Hackney church.

"Who wrote this?"

"No one knows. It was there when we acquired it."

My God, I thought. Maybe de Vere's body could be located and identified. It wasn't in the yard. It was inside the church. It would have been protected there, at least a long while, and the interior was a far smaller space to narrow down the location.

"I don't show this to everyone," the librarian said.
"How many others?"
"Not many. They don't know enough to ask."
"Why me? I didn't ask either."
"Why not," she grinned.

The Yard

The librarian armed me with two arrows in my
research quiver: a photocopy of the burial box under which
de Vere was allegedly buried, assuming he was and is still
there, and a copy of the original St. Augustine floor plan.

I gobbled a quick fish-and-chips wrapped in
vinegared newspaper and acquired the tools I needed at
Woodland's Hardware and Tesco Express. I carted my
equipment and library copies across Mare Street, circled
around behind the tower and sat on a bench that straddled a
paved path that ran along what would have been the north
wall of the old church. I laid my tools on the bench and
turned the floor plan in the direction that mirrored the
tower to my left and the long side of the church directly in
front.

I flipped open six, white paper bags, stood them
upright in a semicircle around my feet and weighted them
down with handfuls of potting stones. I stood and carried
two weighted bags to the back edge of the tower and sat
one at my best guess for the church's northwest corner and
the second at the northeast corner. Then I did the same for
the rear cornerstone locations, pacing off distances to
approximate the rectangular floor plan.

When I finished, I sat back on the bench to survey the results. If de Vere's body was interred within the church, and if it was still there, it had to be somewhere within my white-bagged perimeter.

From what the priest had said when he caught me poking around in his churchyard, the original church was demolished when it was too small to hold more than a thousand. The space in front of me looked far too small to hold that many, but then open spaces often do seem smaller.

I eyed a comparison of the floor plan with my markers then reread the handwritten description beneath the burial box.

Believed to be the burial bench of Edward de Vere, 17th Earl of Oxford standing along the back, south-side wall of the Hackney church.

The long south wall of the church would have risen opposite me as I sat on the bench. I stood again and carried my two remaining weighted bags across what would have been the middle of the church and stood in the approximate center of the missing south wall. I then walked off half the distance toward my rear cornerstone bag. Figuring the size of a box slightly larger than a human body, I sat my final bag in the center of my best guess of where that burial bench must have stood.

As I rechecked my distances, several strollers ambled through the park. One asked what I was up to, but the priest didn't reappear and neither did the local constabulary. I photographed my bags from every angle and perspective I could think of. Then I left the yard to climb the rickety Underground platform across Mare Street to ride the train back to London with no idea if what I had accomplished had any value at all.

Scattered Remains

The Japanese have a saying. "If you know something but don't do it, you don't know it." My father put if differently. "Measure twice, cut once, but at least measure." In investigative parlance that means do your research before you tramp out in the field. It saves a lot of wasted time and effort.

The old Hackney church -- St. Augustine – first rose on sanctified ground in the 13th century. By de Vere's demise four centuries later, bodies were scattered and squeezed into wherever space could be found with no particular relationship to a bench or "buried here" plaque tacked to the wall. "Buried here" simply meant "buried somewhere near here," not necessarily directly beneath that marker.

Burial space was at a premium. It was costly. Inside space was more expensive. Like all organizations, St. Augustine was in constant need of a money flow to operate, and burial space was a continuing source of income until inside space ran out. Churchyards could often be expanded. Inside space could not.

In the early days of a church, a plaque to the wall usually referred to a body beneath it but that became increasingly problematic as perimeter space slowly filled and bodies began to migrate toward the center. A more immediate dilemma arose when no floor space remained to sell at all, when all the money that could be made had been made. That is, until some entrepreneurial priest or bishop conceived of an early Manhattan-like solution. When horizontal space runs out, build up, or in the case of the church, dig down. Down was unlimited as long as gravediggers were constantly willing to dig a little deeper, move previous occupants around a bit, and make maximum use of squeeze space at every level. By de Vere's internment in 1604, a twisted labyrinth of layered coffins jammed and hugged each other at every possible level and angle.

Even if all the bodies beneath the old Hackney church – easily hundreds – were exhumed and laid out in rows on the lawn -- there would be no way to identify de Vere without some sort of pendant on his coffin or draped around his neck. But even that was irrelevant. None of those bodies were going to be exhumed and identified. And no bodies were going to be exhumed from Westminster either. De Vere's body, wherever it was, was lost to antiquity. With no body, there was no DNA. With no DNA, there was no physical proof of fatherhood. With no proof of fatherhood, there was no undeniable evidence that Edward de Vere fathered Elizabeth's child or that the existence of that child motivated a name change on the plays. My work in Hackney, such as it was, was finished.

Stamford

My mind turned back to Cecil Burghley. As Elizabeth's chief spy, Lord Treasurer and Master of Wards, Burghley amassed a fortune from known and unknown sources. He initially sank much of it into Cecil House to physically demonstrate his power and influence in London. As that power, wealth and influence grew, so did his building ambitions. He then built Theobalds, a fifty-five acre palatial estate ten miles from London. He later completed a massive, hundred room palatial estate, Burghley House, on thirteen hundred manicured acres bordering the village of Stamford where Burghley had planned a leisurely retirement.

Theobalds was eventually sold and slowly converted to its current 18th century Georgian style. If they returned today, Burghley and his immediate heirs would find themselves wandering about Theobalds' grounds searching for recognizable signs of the estate and gardens they once strolled.

Burghley House, further distant from London, remained in the family until David Cecil, the 6th Burghley Marquis, inherited a huge tax bill and was forced to sell parts of the Burghley art collections to pay what he owed. Determined to avoid repeated sales, he established the Burghley Trust and empowered the trustees to appoint a member of the family to live in and manage the estate and property.

Burghley himself never found the time or opportunity to fully enjoy Burghley House. Retirement was not in him. He died in London with his political boots strapped on tight and had to be carriaged to Stamford for burial under a massive monument in the north chapel of Stamford's St. Martins.

The train ride to Stamford from London's Victoria Station required a switch to a connector line for a late afternoon arrival at the tiny station on the edge of the village. I had rung ahead and booked a room for the night, appropriately at the William Cecil Lodge, then rested for an hour on a huge canopied bed and enjoyed a leisurely dinner of braised lamb, buttered green beans and garlic potatoes. Feeling both rested and restless, I spent the evening wandering the narrow roads and passageways of a sleepy country village that had retained far more of its 16th century charm and character than close-in Hackney, now a clogged and bustling London suburb.

****

Then suddenly, as I topped a ridge, Burghley House gently emerged in front of me like an Elizabethan castle rising in a mist. I stopped on the crest and stood in the midst of a fairy tale fantasy. What kind of man would build such a magnificent structure? What secrets did that man bury there or carry with him to his grave? What did he leave behind?

****

My self-guided tour of Burghley House started in the belly of the elegant monster, in the kitchen. It was described in the guidebook as a constantly churning mix of heat, activity, and deliveries as a dozen bakers, butchers, cooks and cooks' aids scurried about preparing the next meal and the one after that. A rib-vaulted ceiling soared two stories high. Two huge ovens consumed most of the wall in front of me as the only other visitors – an elderly couple and a single woman – joined me.

As the single woman wandered ahead and the elderly couple lingered behind, I found myself alone, or nearly alone, in the Grand Ballroom, described in the guidebook as "pristinely preserved" just as it was in Burghley's day. "Not many here today," I said to the docent sitting on a chair in the corner and keeping a sharp eye on me lest I steal one of the candlesticks.

"Not many all week," she said in a quiet voice, almost a whisper. "It's still early in the season. Are you American?"

"How could you tell?

"That's mostly what we get this early on… You a tourist?"

"Doing research."

"What kind of research."

"On Burghley. On the man. What he had. What he might have known. What he might have left behind."

"About what of left behind?" the docent asked, a sudden interest scooting her to the edge of her chair.

Since I hadn't spoken to anyone about the authorship controversy in days, the slightest interest was all the bait I needed. Halfway through my story, the docent said, "Hold on. Let me get the other ladies in here." In less than two minutes, she had rounded up three others who gathered around and insisted I start from the beginning.

"So what do you expect to find here at Burghley House," one of them asked when I finished.

"Nothing, really," I said. "Anything that might have been of interest, anything Burghley might have written down or kept account of would have been left in Cecil House in London and that's long gone."

"Not entirely," one of the docents said. "A lot of that stuff was brought here. He never lived here but he planned to. There's a whole room in the basement full of papers and records that were carried over."

"What kind of records" I asked, rising on my toes.

"Nobody knows. There's so many, no one's had time to go through them. It takes all we have just to keep this place in order. Going through old records and account books and stacks of old letters is quite low on the priority list."

****

As I rode the train back to London, staring out the window, I was still amazed and surprised at the docents' common knowledge that didn't seem to be common at all. How, after all this time, could some researcher not have painstakingly examined anything and everything that Burghley might have kept or written? Some of it was examined -- the letters De Vere's sent back to his father-in-law from Italy for one. De Vere didn't have them. He sent them. Burghley had them, and someone had made them public record.

Now the question was, what still remained in Burghley's basement pile that hadn't been culled or even looked at? Had Burghley, the master spy and obsessive record keeper, kept any sort of record, account, note or anything related to William Shakespeare, the Shakespeare plays, or anything else that might shed light on the authorship question?

Roots

I had conflicting ideas of where Edward de Vere might be buried, but I did know where he was born and spent his early years before his father died and he became a ward of Cecil Burghley. He was born and reared in Hedingham Castle, the ancestral home of the de Veres going back to 1066 when Aubrey de Vere, the 1st Earl, accompanied William the Conqueror on his Norman invasion. Edward's ancestral roots were French -- as was the de Vere name – although, by Edward's time, the French language had been absorbed into the English, a language about to explode to new heights of beauty and meaning in literature, first under the name "Anonymous," and then under the name "William Shakes-Speare."

I took a late morning train to the tiny town of Colchester, nestled in the rolling hills of the Colne Valley along the ancient Roman road to Cambridge. From Colchester, I grabbed a cab to Hedingham Castle, arriving around ten thirty and asking the driver to return and pick me up around two. There wasn't much to see, but I wanted to see it all and allow enough time to absorb it.

Hedingham's keep – it's living quarters and watchtower -- rose stalwartly on a commanding hill overlooking the valley beneath. Its outer bailey, its furthest defensive perimeter, enclosed a hundred acres of farm and grazing land and the village that supported the castle. The inner bailey, the close-in defense, accommodated stables, work sheds, a barn, a granary, a kitchen, a brewery and a bake house.

The stone keep appeared to have survived the centuries in good shape as I passed through its thick-walled protective gate, and entered the first floor Great Hall. Above me, a massive arch supported the rooms central weigh while high arched windows captured streams of light as the sun crept around the tower and slowly spread its flowing light across a polished stone floor.

A tiered balcony overlooked the Great Hall, from which Edward's father John, the 16th Earl, must have peered down at his growing son before he died when Edward was twelve. Only Edward's father's ghost patrolled these ancient halls now, much as Hamlet's father's ghost haunted the halls of his father's castle.

As I passed through the second and third level, topped the circular staircase and stepped out onto the upper floor, a large-block printed question confronted me.

IS THIS THE ROOM IN WHICH THE AUTHOR
OF THE SHAKESPEARE PLAYS ONCE SLEPT?

My question exactly.

The Matter of the Boy

There was one more side trip remaining on my journey of discovery. A trail that led to the heart of the matter, to the village of Titchfield on England's southern coast.

I took the train to nearby Southampton, a ninety-minute rail ride. From there, I hopped a local bus to Titchfield.

"Where do you want to be dropped," the uniformed driver asked. Apparently, there were options. I could be dropped wherever I wanted.

"Titchfield," I said. "I'm looking for the Abbey,"

Twenty minutes later, he pulled the bus to a stop at the side of the road, cranked the front door open and glanced over his shoulder. "Right over there," he said, nodding toward a curved path that wound through a thicket of oddly trimmed underbrush that abruptly ended at the front facade of a 13th century Abbey set directly in the center of an expansive manicured lawn.

Only the Abbey's long dead occupants accompanied me as I proceeded across an empty lawn, a hot sun beating on my forehead, its shimmering glare quivering across ancient brick and mortar as if offering proof that life once resided there and could somehow be resurrected.

A laminated sign on a stand to the right of the entrance described the crumbling structure's history.

"An austere order of monastic priests founded The Titchfield Abbey in 1222, devoting themselves to scholarship, daily prayer, and a monastic life. When Henry VIII dissolved the order in 1537 he offered the abbey to Thomas Wriothesley as his living quarters. In the late 16th century, Henry Wriothesley, Thomas's grandson and patron of William Shakespeare, resided in the property. Later abandoned, the structure was partially demolished in 1781."

Henry Wriothesley? William Shakespeare's patron? Patron or son, I wondered aloud, but the ghosts of the abbey held their silence. No matter. Whispering of ghosts wouldn't suffice. I needed solid, earthly proof. I needed a corpse. I needed DNA from Henry Wriothesley's body. But if his body was buried somewhere in the abbey yard, there was no marker, telltale protrusions, or any other evidence that would block the passage of a tractor-mower tracing lines across that lawn. I was out of luck with the body of Edward de Vere in Hackney or in Westminster, I had no chance of resurrecting the Queen from her long Westminster sleep, and now my luck had run out with Henry Wriothesley. I was out of luck all around as I headed along the path that lead toward the village steeple.

****

The trail that led me behind the village church, as is usually the case for Elizabethan sanctuaries, passed through a graveyard with 17th and 18th century names and dates etched on most of their stones, while others, pitted and pot marked, defied attempts to discern any information from their dents and depressions. If Wriothesley was buried in the Titchfield churchyard, perhaps at least there might be church records to indicate names and locations. But even if there were, what condition would four hundred years of wind and water leave on a body buried beneath?

Unlike London churches, mostly locked against street vandals, village churches still trusted their parishioners. The wooden double door of Titchfield's St. Peter's Episcopal stood wide open, inviting those in who sought a respite for prayer or contemplation, although no one had availed themselves of that opportunity as I entered quietly and slipped into a rear pew to contemplate my own disappointing situation.

It was then that God answered a prayer I hadn't known I'd made. I heard something stirring up front and leaned toward a shadow in a side chapel. As I stood and eased down a side aisle, whoever or whatever it was apparently hadn't noticed me.

As I rounded a corner and peeked over a rail, the ample backside of a woman waddled atop the second tier of a fifteen-foot high monument, stretching a long-handled feather duster as high as she could and sweeping its' tip across the prone effigy of a body.

"What!" the woman exclaimed and she twisted around, startled as she glared down at me. "I didn't mean to…"

"Neither did I," I said.

"They leave the door open." She nodded toward the front. "Dust flies in all day."

"That must keep you busy up there."

"The Wriothesleys. They always were a lot of trouble."

"The Wriothesleys? I'm looking for a Wriothesley."

"Which one," she said, climbing down and dusting off her apron.

"Henry Wriothesley. The 3rd Earl."

"Well, you've found him. You're standing on him." She stooped next to the monument and touched her finger to the raised likeness of a boy holding a tray.

"He's buried here?"

"Right under you. There's a tomb down there. It's full of Wriothesleys."

"How do you know that? Is there a record?"

She shrugged. "I supposed. The historical society would know. They keep track of those sorts of things."

****

As it turned out, the historical society didn't know, at least not precisely. They knew there were Wriothesleys entombed inside the church. After all, it was the Wriothesley monument. They just weren't sure how many. Some thought five. Others, maybe seven. But one of them, all agreed, was Henry Wriothesley, the 3rd Earl of Southampton.

It didn't take long for word to spread that a stranger was snooping around the village, skulking around graves and asking a lot of questions. When I arrived back at the Bugle Inn, the innkeeper handed me a note inviting me for tea at three to meet with several members of the historical committee who would be most pleased if I accepted. The offer felt more like a sheriff's invitation but that was fine with me. They wanted to learn who I was and I wanted to learn a few things from them.

The committee confirmed, over tea and a lot of nods and head shakes, that three generations of Wriothesley's were interred beneath the church floor, one of them a child who died in infancy. One committee member recalled a survey conducted in 1937 when a corner of the floor began to sink under the massive weigh of the monument and the entrance stone beneath the organ was removed to allow entry in order to reinforce the support beams.

"The coffins were apparently haphazardly stacked," the committee member recalled. "But they were still all closed and clearly labeled. They were encased in honey, I believe. A good preservative. They should be in good condition, however good that might be after four hundred years."

I recalled what the "old bones" expert from the University of Pennsylvania had told me when I asked about a DNA sample. "Get me a wisdom tooth," she had said, "and I can make a match from that. If the sample matched the DNA of the deceased's mother or grandmother or any other female back along that maternal line, then the deceased, the boy, would be the son of the final mother."

But even if I could dig up Wriothesley's body and it

was well preserved and clearly identified, how could I dig up someone along Queen Elizabeth's maternal bloodline? Whatever additional research I needed to do on that score, would have to wait for later.

I had piqued the Titchfield Historic Committee's interest. "Listen," I told them at a hastily convened evening meeting. "If Henry Wriothesley turns out the be the son of Queen Elizabeth, and if that son is buried right here in Titchfield, and if that leads to the identification of the Queen's lover as the author of the Shakespeare plays, you need to start planning parking lots for tour buses before the hoards start pouring in. You need to do so before that discovery is made."

While the Historic Committee considered the implications of my outrageous contention, they assigned one of their trusted members -- Barry Ruck, a short-statured curmudgeon with a quick sense of humor and an infectious smile – to keep tabs on me and report back any trouble I might be stirring up. But I took to Barry right away and he took to me. Instead of spying on me, we partnered.

"The bishop wants to speak with us," Barry informed me. The word had spread wide. Now, it was filtering up. "He's rearranged his schedule," Barry added. "He wants to meet us in his upstairs office at St. Peters at four thirty."

At four thirty precisely, I sat across from a double-chinned, white-collared priest while Barry sat behind as I attempted to explain why I was there and what I was looking for. I had hardly begun when the bishop raised a flattened palm to stop me. "So, if I understand what you're asking," he began, obviously well informed of my intent and its implications, "you want to exhume Henry Wriothesley's body, extract a DNA sample and replace him in the tomb. Is that about it?"

"That's exactly it."

"Well, then I can emphatically inform you as directly as I can, that will never happen. I would never approve and the archbishop clearly would not. It would have to go that high. Is that it? Is there anything else I can do for you?"

"No. That should do it."

"God be with you then."

As I staggered back down the steps and out in the churchyard, Barry caught up and walked alongside. "It's going to take a lot of prayers to overcome that," I said.

"Not necessarily," Barry said. "Let me translate what just happened back there. You can't break into consecrated ground. The church would never permit that. And the church doesn't take bribes either. But here's the situation. Church attendance is way down all over England. The young don't attend like their parents and grandparents did. And then there's all that upkeep on all those old buildings. But let's say you were to make a reasonable contribution to the roofing fund. Say something on the order of two thousand American dollars. There's a good chance that body would float right up out of there."

The BBC

I eventually earned a Ph.D. in psychology, but I started out with an undergraduate major in television production and worked for a while at ABC and the U.S. Information Agency. ABC was always on the lookout for what they called "great TV," which meant controversy, especially conspiratorial. When a producer smelled a rat, we dug our cameras out and followed that scent back to a nest, then rattled a stick around in that hole and waited to see what emerged.

I had a day free before my ticket home and I definitely smelled a rat. If the four-hundred-year-old authorship question amounted to a cover-up and a conspiracy of silence, it would be the greatest and most successful literary conspiracy in history. That's the kind of rat scent a TV producer might want to grab a stick and follow.

I dressed in a jacket and tie, the only one I'd brought, checked to make sure I had a professional business card in my wallet, then trotted down to London's BBC Central and clipped up the front steps as if I owned the place. I aimed directly for the front desk, stretched the most authoritative smile I could muster as I handed my business card to the receptionist and announced, "I'm a clinical psychologist. I have an idea for a show that involves conspiracy and the queen." I didn't say which queen. "Is there a producer around I could speak with?"

"Have a seat over there." She nodded toward an array of leather chairs in groups of four.

In less than five minutes, an elevator opened, a

three-piece-suit, twenty-something emerged and approached the receptionist who nodded in my direction.

"Dr. Hutchison," he asked, glancing at my card as I stood. "How can I help you?"

He sat across from me, nodding and listening as I spent the next twenty minutes detailing why I was there. "Is this something you might have an interest in," I asked at the end.

"You're writing a book on this," he asked, wisely sensing my intent.

I told him that I was.

"Let me keep your card," he said as he reached in his pocket and handed me his. "Let's keep in touch. We might very well be interested. We could follow you down to Titchfield as they exhumed the body and extracted a tooth. And, if they refused, if they blocked the door, we could film you standing in front the church claiming a four hundred year old cover-up. That's great TV."

"That's exactly what I thought."

Home

The flight home was a let down. There was nothing more to do or see. Nothing more, that is, but relive the adventure as I wrote it. But this time not entirely for myself. This time for Edward de Vere, the 17th Earl of Oxford, the man whose life and footsteps I had followed across the south of England. This time I wanted to get a feel, as close I could, for what it must have been like to be Edward de Vere, to experience his joys and anguish and the devastation he must have felt to have his name stripped from a lifelong labor of love.

A little over a year later, I leaned back with a sigh of relief. I had traveled a long-forgotten path twice. I had lived it twice. And now I had written it for others to live. Here is the result. The first two chapters follow.

LOVE'S LABOR LOST

The Man Who Was Shakespeare

The Winds of Conspiracy

> "Affection is a coal that must be cool'd --
> Else, suffer'd, it will set the heart on fire."
> *Venus and Adonis, Stanza 65*

Elizabethan England
The Road to Windsor Castle
Mid Winter, 1623

One might assume the winter snows would have cooled the hot winds of conspiracy. Not so this frozen winter day. As the heavy snow of February blinded galloping horses whose hooves cracked the ice along the road to Windsor Castle, royal hands warmed before Windsor's huge hearth as thoughts of deception stoked its flames. "But at what price the realm?" James I, the King of England, thought as he drew his palms back from the heat, although he well knew the price, or at least suspected it.

Susan Herbert, her steeds plowing through a frozen mist that flared their nostrils, had no problem with secrecy or the price of deception. Beyond her husband, the Earl of Montgomery, she had confided in no one, certainly not in matters of this gravity, and especially not in the affairs of court. Had it not been the court's duplicity that had brought England to this regrettable day?

Susan herself was not above deceit and deception, or beyond ruse piled upon innuendo to cloak the truth buried beneath. She had learned from the master -- her father. When times required action, nay, when they *demanded* action -- "Act," she whispered to herself as her coach struck a frozen stump, lifted her delicate body from the seat, and slammed it back down.

Susan's hands trembled in her lap. As the coach settled again, she clutched her knees to hold them still and steady her nerves. The meeting ahead of her would be the most important of her life. It would determine a life or a death. She leveled her shoulders, leaned forward, poked a gloved finger through the curtain, and peeked outside. She was running late. Axle-high snowdrifts slowed her passage over Chads Forge and for several leagues along the road to Birnum, but the sight of Windsor's soaring towers reassured her that they were nearly there.

The sight of Windsor pulled her thoughts back to Hedingham Castle, to a girl of seven laying belly-down before the hearth, staring eye-level through the gate of a miniature village her father had constructed, much like the village of Colne at the foot of Hedingham Castle, the ancestral home of the de Vere family and the place where her father had been raised and where she spent much time as a child. She still had visions of the miniature knights and painted toy soldiers marching under tiny thatched overhangs, shuffled along by the push of her thumb. She recalled picking up the figure of a charwoman or a blacksmith between her small fingers, turning them to face each other and then speaking on their behalf, lowering her voice or raising it to suit the character. And she remembered her father playing a part, squealing in falsetto to exaggerate a maiden, then lowering his voice to mock an arrogant prince or bishop, and then falling out of character, laughing and rolling on the floor pounding his fists at his own embellishments. Pretense, Susan thought as she drew her attention back to the meeting before her. The essence of deceit posing as reality.

Phillip, Susan's husband, had participated in the plot and provided its financing. Yet, this final step, that which would conceal the truth forever, had been left to Susan, at age thirty-six -- a short-statured, thin-boned woman. And why not a woman? Had not the last monarch been a woman? Had she not sat longer and stronger on the throne than any monarch before her? Had she not launched the flotilla that defeated the Spanish Armada? Had she not spread and cultivated the seeds that spawned the most prolific increase in English literature the world had ever known, and had not that very proliferation set the stage for Susan's father, the creator of a body of work so explosive in its implication that its obliteration was now royal command?

Susan's horses balked at Windsor's drawbridge, impatiently digging in their hooves as melting snow trickled down their haunches, their power barely restrained by the thinnest of harnesses. As soon as the drawbridge thumped down and clanked into place, the steeds bolted forward without encouragement from the whip, rattling over oak planks and thundering beneath a brick archway before rumbling across cobblestone into a walled courtyard. As the horseman heaved the reins back, the coachman leveraged his rawhide brake against the spin of the wheels, skidding the coach to a stop.

Susan, donning leather britches, unusual even for her, tucked her rabbit-fur collar close around her neck, flung the coach door open, and hopped into ankle-deep snow before the coach's springs had fully settled. She glanced over her shoulder and nodded toward the chest strapped to the coach's boot. The coachman hopped down and elbowed snow from the chest's ribs, unbuckled its straps, and lugged it forward, trailing Susan up steps worn smooth by four centuries of royal visits before passing through double doors and into the massive hall of St. George. The coachman, his body still trembling from the wind and their haste, plunked his burden down at Susan's feet, knocking off chunks of ice that melted on the stone floor, then departed without further instruction, the slam of the doors behind him echoing down the long hall in search of a crack or a crevice in which to hide, and finding none, dissipating in the thick weave of tapestries that draped from the vaulted ceiling.

When all lay quiet, a tiny portal set within a larger door creaked open and a man with a baldhead poked through. His eyes swept down the hall and fixed on Susan before he opened the crack wide enough to enter. "His Highness inquires if you are alone in your presence, Madam," he asked, more breathe than voice.

Susan stiffened her spine to strengthen her resolve. "Quite alone," she said.

The man stooped and unsnapped a lower latch, then straightened and opened a second latch higher up, and one at a time, unfolded two sides of an enormous hinged door, releasing heat that swooped into the entrance hall and flushed Susan's face, still chilled from the cold. The immense silhouette of a man stood between Susan and a crackling inferno that consumed the wall behind him. Satan himself, Susan thought.

"You brought them?" the man's voice boomed, although in the shadowed darkness she barely saw his lips move.

She spread her palm toward the trunk at her feet.

"*All* of them?"

"As agreed."

"And the copies?"

"Here as well." She slid a parchment out from inside her coat and held it forward. "The inventory," she said.

"Leave it."

She pivoted and laid the document on the round of the trunk, the melting ice immediately staining it. "And the burial?" she asked, turning to face the man again.

"Reburial," he corrected her, then paused, his voice softer. He stepped toward her, growing taller and wider as he approached. "He would have conceded this a necessary sacrifice," he reassured her. "You are simply doing what is necessary in his stead."

"You'll destroy them then? You'll commit them to flames?" Susan asked as a log crackled and split in the fire, although Susan held a risky proposal in the back of her mind -- a deceitful, even treacherous alternative -- yet one that might fulfill her secret hope and still keep England from a renewed upheaval that could split the realm down its religious seams.

CHAPTER 2

Fire in the Night

"O, who can hold fire in his hand?"
Richard II, I, 3

Fifty-two Years Earlier
The 17th of August, in the Year of Our Lord 1558
Hedingham Castle near the village of Colne

The chapel bells clanged furiously. John de Vere, the Sixteenth Earl of Oxford, sprung up in bed, his heart thumping, sweat bleeding down his chest. Night bells bespoke one thing. *Fire!* At a bang on his door, he catapulted up and dashed across the cold stone floor.

"Your Lordship!" a high-pitched voice shouted through the cracks. "The theater! 'Tis a'fire!"

The Earl wrenched the door open and burst into the hall, racing behind a shorter, red-haired man who scampered ahead like a limp rabbit, hopping and stretching his right foot forward, then angling his left to catch up. By the time they darted across the great hall and flew into the west courtyard, flames had already spread from beam to beam across the roof of the old stables the Earl had converted into an outdoor stage for his theatrical productions.

The Earl, his eyes ablaze in the reflected fire, clutched the wooden rake thrust into his hand and joined the fray as a score of shadowed men dashed in and out of the flames, beating them back with brooms and horse-hair blankets whilst woman and boys sloshed buckets hand-to-hand from the central well.

By the first glint of sunlight, the inferno had banked to embers as scorched-faced men lay scattered on the ground, the bravest of them, when the fire began, having rushed in to pinch it back until falling timbers drove them out.

Slumped against the warm wall of the keep, the lingering smoke coating his throat and burning his nostrils, the Earl half-lifted his eyes as an aproned maid offered him water, his cracked lips able to absorb only a few drops. His face blistered, his legs spattered in mud, he rolled his eyes toward his manservant hunched over beside him. "Plunkin," the Earl whispered in a hoarse voice.

"Sire?" Plunkin answered without raising his chin, as if too exhausted to lift it from his chest.

"How did it begin, Plunkin?"

"I…" Plunkin hesitated. "I know not, Sire."

"Plunkin?"

"I shan't say for certain."

"You *shan't,* but you could."

"I might have seen a shadow."

"Whose might it be?"

"A slender shadow."

"Slender?… Slender as…?"

"I can only guess, Sire."

The Earl fixed his stare.

"I believe… I can only surmise," Plunkin said,

avoiding his master's gaze. "It may have been… It may have been your own. The young Earl."

****

"What are we to do with the likes of him?" an exasperated Lady Margaret cried. A tall, hollow-cheeked woman who habitually peered down upon her husband, Lady Margaret rose on her toes to further her height advantage when she wished to hammer a point into her husband's skull and twist it there until he admitted fault and acknowledged her position. As to the matter of their son, Edward, the Earl had abandoned all defense as he cowered on a bench while his wife paced over him, halting and lengthening her neck every time she turned, her fingers poking forth and flicking about like an angry hawk whose nest was being invaded. Lady Margaret would have her way. The price weighed too heavy if she did not.

"He needs…," the Earl began, unsure what to say, yet realizing a response was required. The problem was, he reluctantly agreed with his wife. The boy habitually yanked a dog's tail simply to see if it wagged the animal's body. He oft disappeared in the forest for hours, frightening the household for his safety and then denying it with one of his fanciful tales. He would plead he was pursued by one of his imaginary characters -- a warlock, or an evil fairy-queen, or his favorite, a three-horned, web-footed, green goblin he called Hornthrust, a devilish beast the boy claimed hounded him into the woods, begetting trouble there, then laying blame at Edward's feet knowing he would not be believed. Edward frustrated his father, although John well knew that whatever correction he imposed to discipline his son would not be enough to please his wife. She was rarely pleased when wheels spun smoothly and not at all with the least squeak. "I'm certain he had his reason," the Earl offered limply.

Lady Margaret threw her hands above her head and clawed the air, exaggerating emotion like the actors John employed. *"Reason?"* Lady Margaret mocked John's voice. "For *burning* down the theater in yet another of his outrageous make-believes? 'Tis precisely what leads him astray in the first place."

The Earl agreed with that as well, though he chose silence, his admissions often self-incriminating and calling forth another blade to further stab him. "The pebble rolls not far from the stone," Lady Margaret liked to say.

Lady Margaret rose on her toes and glared down at the shiniest spot atop her husband's balding head. "You *haven't* spoken to him, have you?"

"I've been weighing my words. I *shall* speak with him directly."

She spit breath through her tightened lips, as she frequently did to dismiss her husband or anyone else with whom she disagreed.

Edward bore a pain in his mother's side from the moment of his birth, although that hardly explained her distaste for others, her husband atop the list. She had screamed her son into this world and then blamed John for planting the seed that spawned him. Edward, or so the chambermaids reported, poked his head from his mother's womb and refused to continue, holding there as if to change his mind and crawl back in. Worse, when he did grudgingly exit, he seemed to grin, taunting his mother, knowing the poor woman had suffered through a twelve-hour labor. Thus enraged, when Margaret lurched to grab the babe's throat, the chambermaids caught his slippery afterbirth and pulled him away to save his life. To stab injury deeper, the infant developed colic, his wail echoing through Hedingham's halls, rousing servants and parents alike throughout the night.

At Margaret's insistence, Juliana -- a chambermaid suckling her own newborn -- took Edward to her quarters to allow Milady to rest and regain her strength. Unable to sleep himself, the Earl sneaked down to the servant's quarters to hold his son, reciting poetry to lull him to sleep.

"You've been with Juliana, have you not?" Margaret asked the next morning.

"Not *with* her. I could not sleep. I heard him cry."

"You've always found Juliana fair."

"The maid?... I take no notice of Juliana."

"You say her name with such relish. It sweetly rolls from your tongue."

"She's a pleasant sort, nothing more."

"Oh?... And I am *not?*"

"Of course you are, my dear."

"Don't lie to me. I know what they say."

"Pay no mind to them."

"So you agree, then... You and your son are of the same ilk."

"Our son."

"*You* are the one who required an heir. If I had not watched him creep from my womb, I should not be certain he was mine. He is more suited to Julianna's kind. Of her kind."

"Margaret, that's absurd."

"Or that other bitch."

The Earl knew Margaret would soon wind her way to this. She always did. She was referring neither to Juliana nor to his first wife, now deceased. She meant Mistress Dorothy, the woman in between, the woman the Earl might have married and perhaps should have, he thought as a grin escaped his lips. He *did* marry a bitch. She simply wasn't Mistress Dorothy.

"What's that smirk of?" Margaret asked. "You find this amusing?"

"Not at all," he lied, flattening his expression. The subject of Mistress Dorothy would never be settled, nor would the proper education of Edward, although of that, the Earl was less concerned. The boy read voraciously, spoke three languages at the age of eight, and had well taken up the sword. He rode and hunted, if not as the best, fair better than the least. All came readily. *Too* readily. He studied naught, absorbing knowledge as easily as he parried the sword. What the boy knew not, he spoke of so convincingly as to tangle truth with cleverness.

Edward bored easily and feared nothing, the theatre fire merely his latest indiscretion, although John conceded it more destructive than his usual pranks. Should the boy set his itchy feet upon firmer ground, perhaps he *could* manage the Earldom one day. There would be no other children, Lady Margaret having refused the Earl to her bed after Edward's birth. Edward, their only son, would *be* the next Earl, yet discipline would be required to reign in his rebellious nature, harness his fantasies, and redirect his attention to the road ahead and away from the birds and butterflies in the fields, half of which flew only in his head.

"And *now* the fire," Margaret said, raising her voice and seizing the opportunity to dig her claws in deeper. "It's time we considered sending him off."

"We can't abandon a boy of eight," the Earl protested, shaking his head without glancing up.

"Perhaps north," Margaret said. "To your cousin Manfred. When we sent him those unruly hounds, he made the better of them."

"He needs to remain with us. To experience running the estates."

"The estates?" Margaret tightened her jaw. "They run themselves. There is naught for *you* to do, let alone your lazy son."

"Margaret," John pleaded. "I don't…"

"England has changed," she interrupted, her hands inching close enough to reach down and strangle him. "Our insipid former king, that knave Henry, brought us to this. We became one nation under Henry. The warring castles that once fought each other now meet in Parliament to shake their fists and adjourn to trade jokes over grog. Warriors? There is not a knightly man among them. The barons and earls are no longer fighters. You are all farmers. There is nothing left to defend, nothing to pass onto your ne'er-do-well son but a worthless title and lands that bring naught but worry and expense." When Margaret paused, John felt the heat of her gaze permeate down his spine. He had heard this all before, though not quite this vehemently. He knew his best defense against her siege was silence. "And what will your worthless son *do?* Have you thought of that? There *is* nothing for him to do, save burn down the next theater you build out of your own frivolity."

****

"Why did you set the fire, son?"

"I did not, father."

"Plunkin saw you."

"I didn't set it, father. It caught on fire."

"What were you doing out there?"

"Playing a part."

The Earl's chest sunk in frustration.

"A play came to me whilst in bed," Edward said, eying his father cautiously. "I was playing the part on stage, marking off the actors."

"In the middle of the night?"

"I could not sleep. I went to the theatre to act upon it. I needed a torch for the light."

"Son..." The Earl hesitated. "Your mother and I have reached a decision. That is to say, 'tis I who've decided."

END OF CHAPTER TWO

The remainder of the sad and exciting story of the life of Edward de Vere – AKA William Shakespeare – is available for purchase online.

About the Author

Dr. Bruce Hutchison earned a Master's Degree in psychology from Stanford University and his Ph.D. in psychology from Maryland the University of Maryland. He was the Chief Psychologist at a Maryland Mental Health Center, a graduate college instructor and counselor at Washington College and maintained a thriving private practice in Easton, Maryland. Bruce has worked as an evaluator and consultant for the Maryland Court System and for local police departments, in addition to providing testimony as an expert witness and psychological profiler for both the prosecution and the defense. He was a longtime member of the State of Maryland's Forensic Evaluation Team. He is a frequent speaker and workshop presenter for community groups, churches, and professional conferences in the United States and around the world. He is married and lives both in Santa Fe, New Mexico and in Annapolis, Maryland, although he frequently travels, presenting seminars, talks and lectures.

CPSIA information can be obtained at www.ICGtesting.com
Printed in the USA
BVOW08s1226071215

429597BV00001B/15/P